TEXTILES
FOR YOU

Elaine and John Pomeroy

Hutchinson

London Melbourne Auckland Johannesburg

Hutchinson Education

An imprint of Century Hutchinson Ltd

62–65 Chandos Place, London WC2N 4NW

Century Hutchinson Australia Pty Ltd
PO Box 496, 16–22 Church Street, Hawthorn,
Melbourne, Victoria 3122, Australia

Century Hutchinson New Zealand Ltd
PO Box 40-086, Glenfield, Auckland 10,
New Zealand

Century Hutchinson South Africa (Pty) Ltd
PO Box 337, Bergvlei, 2012 South Africa

First published 1988

Design by Heather Richards
Technical illustrations by Taurus Graphics
Cartoons by Kate Charlesworth

Typeset in Monophoto Helvetica by
Vision Typesetting, Manchester

Printed in Great Britain by
Butler & Tanner Ltd, Frome and London

British Library Cataloguing in Publication Data
Pomeroy, Elaine
  Textiles for you.
  1. Textiles – For schools
  I. Title II. Pomeroy, John
  677
ISBN 0-09-172471-6

Introduction

This book is aimed at the requirements for textiles teaching in GCSE syllabuses including Textiles Studies and Home Economics–Textiles. It should also be useful to Art and Design students requiring greater understanding of textiles materials and the design concept and on BTec courses with similar aims.

The emphasis is on the total textiles area as required by the design process approach which integrates aesthetics, performance, practical and economic considerations and relates to the contemporary consumer market in clothing and household items and to industrial usage.

The text shows how the subject may be used to forward the aims of the proposed National Core Curriculum in art and design, applied science and technology, mathematics, and its relation to the world of industry and commerce.

To meet the requirements of the GCSE assessment the book includes higher level work designated by ⚑ . These could be used in total, included on a second reading only or omitted altogether by some pupils. Each chapter includes a summary, questions at varying levels and design briefs which could form the basis of coursework assessment for examination purposes.

Contents

1

Why do we wear clothes?

This book is about textiles. We all use textiles in a number of different ways – some perhaps that you did not realize. The sort of textile products everyone is familiar with are clothes. We all wear them, but have you ever thought why?

If you were asked to say why you wore clothes, you would probably come up with three reasons which could be put down as:

1 To look good
2 To be 'decent'
3 To keep warm

– even if you did not use these exact words. Let us look at these three points in more detail and they will tell us a lot more about clothes.

1.1 Social conventions

We will start with being 'decent' and ask ourselves the question – what does being decent mean?

Covering up parts of the body that should not be shown, even when it is quite warm enough to go without clothes, may be what we think of as being decent. But let's look at this further.

Firstly, who decides what is right or wrong, what is decent or indecent? Secondly, what is considered decent varies depending on where you are – you might wear a bikini or swimming briefs on the beach, but you would not wear them in a restaurant in the town (would you?). Thirdly, you might not wear a bikini at all – some people are prepared to bathe naked, whilst others consider a bikini indecent. So the question of what is 'right' or 'wrong', what is 'good' or 'bad' in the way we behave, also applies to the clothes we wear.

For every society and culture there are customs which may go back a long way. Many are influenced by religion and sometimes they may become law so that you are punished in some way if you break the law. These customs can also affect the way people dress. Contrast the virtually naked bodies of certain Indian tribes in the Amazon area of South America with the totally covered bodies of women in strict Muslim cultures where no features are clearly visible, and garments are big and flowing to hide the shape of the human body. In the United Kingdom and Europe, clothing was for a long time dominated by the Christian church, which generally meant that the body was covered and hidden as much as possible – we still see examples of this today in nuns' clothing and the restrictions on visitors to Roman Catholic cathedrals like St Peter's in Rome – you cannot go in with bare shoulders or exposed legs.

Gradually, as religious beliefs changed, restrictions on what could be shown in public also changed. In Victorian times the bosom could be fairly well exposed, but it was thought terribly indecent if a woman showed even the smallest part of her legs and feet. Rich women in Victorian times wore a crinoline skirt which was so big that it kept men at arm's length. Contrast this sort of skirt with the mini skirt of the 1960s which showed just about every part of the leg! Such a skirt would never have been permitted by church authorities when religion controlled people's lives. We see then that what people wear – fashion, if you like – depends on what is happening to social conditions in the world around us.

But social ideas don't just influence clothes in terms of covering up parts of the body; they influence the sorts and styles of clothes that we wear. For example, what about the skirt? We generally think that skirts are worn by women and the only changes are how long or short they are, but skirts for men? – that doesn't seem 'right' – or does it? In some societies, skirts or garments rather like them are normal wear for men, indeed they can be a sign of importance. Think of the Scottish kilt and the traditional dress of Arabian men.

And what about trousers? For many years they have been the dress of men in Western culture, but not thought right for women. Yet in some societies a trouser-like garment is traditional for women. Nowadays in Western society women wear trousers as much as skirts: denim jeans, for example.

Social custom not only affects the sort of everyday garments we wear, but in particular what it is thought right or wrong to wear on special occasions, such as a wedding, a funeral, or religious ceremonies. For example, most cultures have a traditional garment worn by brides. In Western culture this is the traditional white wedding dress. But it wasn't always white. In medieval times it was often red, because red was thought to scare off demons.

There are social customs for all sorts of

things, from school uniforms to what you
should wear for playing tennis, and they are
always changing.

It is important to realize that just as the
way we live our lives – our **social conventions**
– change, so the sorts of things we wear
on different occasions change. Whenever a
form of dress that has been around for a
long time changes, there are many people
who make a big fuss about the change and
say – 'the world is falling apart' or 'things
will never be the same again' or something
similar. Equally, there are people who
deliberately wear different sorts of clothes
to show that they disapprove of social
conventions – like hippies in the 1970s and
punks in the 1980s – while some people
wear different clothes just because they
want to be noticed. And that brings us on to
another reason for wearing clothes –
looking good, or rather looking good as we
see it.

1.2 **Looking good**

Once again, we have to ask ourselves a question. What do we mean by looking good? Looking good for whom – ourselves or for other people?

We have seen in the last section how strong social influence can be on what is 'right' or 'wrong' to wear, and depending on the sort of person you are you may feel uncomfortable if you are wearing what people think is wrong for a certain occasion. On the other hand, you might like to shock, in which case you would presumably be quite happy.

Once you have satisfied the basic social rules, there is still a lot of variety that you can introduce into your clothes; plenty of ways of expressing your individuality, which is what clothes are all about. But again, most people dress not just for themselves, but in order to be accepted by other people. Parents at first have a strong influence, although as you get older that becomes less important. Teenagers, for example, may be much more influenced by their friends and associates – who are termed their peer group. You like to feel you are in with the crowd, one of the gang, and dress accordingly. That may give way to dressing for your partner – boyfriend or girlfriend. In the end you try to give yourself a fashion **'look'** – part of your **image** – and that is the view people have of you as a complete person.

But one thing is certain: what you wear is constantly changing. This is because **fashion** – what it is thought right to wear in a particular place at a particular time – is always changing.

Why do things change? Many people feel that old values are best, but at the same time, if we say somebody is 'old fashioned' we don't think of that as a compliment. What is it that makes fashions change? Many people have tried to work this out and many societies have tried to stop it happening because they believe it shows a wrong attitude to the way we live. In China, when the Communists came to power in 1950, it

was decided that the most important tasks were overcoming economic problems, and that dress was a frivolity and fashion could be dispensed with. So everybody, regardless of their position in society or whether they were men or women, wore the same basic dull-coloured tunic and trousers and soft peaked cap. Other Communist parties have said that fashion is simply a capitalist way of taking money from workers. Some feminists also believe that fashion is wrong because it turns women into display objects, only interested in decoration and consequently fit only for decoration.

But despite all this, fashion marches on. The papers, television and magazines still contain fashion news, and people are still

△ Brent Cross Shopping Centre, London

interested. Many fashion shops continue to do well, and people still buy far more clothes than they need, because they want to stay in fashion.

Why is this? Many reasons have been put forward – here are some of them

1 When people are changing their jobs and changing their position in society (perhaps getting richer), they like to show other people that this is happening, and dressing fashionably is a way of doing so (along with buying a flashy motor car).

2 Some people have more money to spend than others, and they can indulge their taste for luxury items, clothes being amongst these.

3 People have more leisure time and therefore have more time to spend looking at clothes, which makes them want new fashions.

4 People travel more, experience different cultures, see clothes which they have never seen before and feel they too would like to wear them.

5 More people play sports and like to show that they do so not just by wearing the clothes to play the game, but by wearing clothes associated with the game (such as track suits).

6 Advances in technology bringing the new fibres which have appeared since the 1950s have meant new types of fabric (such as stretch denim) which, for example, make clothes easier to care for and give new fashion effects. These, again, can make people want more clothes.

7 People are often influenced by the famous – royals, sports people, film and pop stars – and copy the way they dress, thus starting new fashions.

8 Finally, deliberate fashion change is brought about by business. The textile industry relies on people buying more clothes than they need, and given the opportunity will seize on new ideas, promote them by advertising and hope to start a fashion.

If fashion is so important, what does it consist of? It can mean a whole new type of garment for a particular group of people – like hotpants in the early 1970s. More often, it means changes of style to established garments, such as shorter skirts or flared bottoms on trousers. It can also mean a change of colour. Some colours, like white, black, blue and red, go on and on, but now and then certain fashion colours appear which are worn a lot for a while and then disappear.

Fashion changes have, of course, been going on for centuries (for those who could afford them), and over the years what people have worn in many cultures has changed dramatically.

So who does make fashion change? That is indeed a question, and if clothing manufacturers knew the answer they would be very happy because they would be able to make a lot of money predicting with certainty what fashion was next going to occur. For many people, fashion comes from a few designers, often famous names who come up with an idea which everybody accepts. The centre of the fashion world is often seen as being Paris, but there are plenty of designers working all over the world, including London, and they are by no means all French or British, but are of all nationalities. Here is a list of some famous designers of the twentieth century.

Coco Chanel – French
Pierre Balmain – French
Christian Dior – French
Yves St Laurent – French
Mary Quant – British
Hardy Amies – British
Norman Hartnell – British

But famous designers have not always been right in what they have predicted in fashion. Some of them became famous because one of their ideas came off. This tells us something about designers. They cannot just dictate fashion; people will only accept it if it is what they want and goes along with what they feel is right. A good designer is someone who looks at the fashion scene, sees what change might be possible and that people will accept it, and then finds the right material and puts their idea on the market in such a way that people see it and buy it.

Fashion, too, is international. What is often called Western fashion may spread all over the world. This is certainly true in places like Japan where the traditional dress worn by both men and women right up to the 1950s has very definitely disappeared in everyday life, particularly amongst men, and Western-style business dress is now normal. But traditional Japanese style often appears as a fashion feature all around the world. The result is that so-called Western culture and Western fashion are being influenced by styles from other cultures, and fashion is therefore becoming completely international.

Here are some fashions from non-European cultures which have influenced world fashion in recent years.

poncho – from Mexico
sari – from India
kimono – from Japan
headbands – from India
'Afghan' coats – from Afghanistan

One point about fashion is that we either like it or we don't. Why we wear something is a personal choice. We call this a **subjective** judgement. We respond to fashion by the look, the feel, the shape, the colour – by things which are not easy to measure. We can believe that these, more than anything else, are the reasons why we wear clothes. But, as we have seen, our particular mixture of traditional and social values and a desire either to be different or to be accepted, all play an important part.

1.3 Uniforms

One of the things to note about fashion is that, although we like to be fashionable, that is, the same as other people, we don't like to find ourselves dressed exactly the same

as others on a social occasion – like turning up to a wedding in the same outfit as a friend.

But there are occasions and occupations where people do wear exactly the same clothes – we call these uniforms. Uniforms are used so that people can feel part of the same group and other people can recognize that they are.

Here are some examples:

1 A uniform helps other people to recognize somebody's authority or position, such as a policeman, or airline crew. The uniform tells you who they are and what they do.
2 It allows members of the same group to recognize that you are one of them. This was the old idea of the military uniform, so that you could recognize who was your friend and who was your enemy in battle. It applies to any team game, such as football.
3 It makes members of the same group feel together; for example, youth organizations like scouts, or any sort of club blazer.
4 It stops people dressing in extremes – this is one of the arguments in favour of school uniforms, that it is better for all pupils to wear the same so that children of rich parents do not look vastly different from those of parents who are not so well off.

We all know the sort of special uniform that we have just talked about, but sometimes everyday clothing can become uniform. When the big fashion for denim was at its height, so many people were wearing denim that it almost became a uniform for a large part of the population. At social events, when men wear evening dress, again this is like a uniform, because they all wear almost exactly the same clothes.

1.4 Protection

One of the reasons for wearing clothes is keeping warm. Now of course, that doesn't

but we should. We expect our clothes to last a reasonable time, and be able to be cleaned (usually washed), and these things don't just happen by chance; they have to be built into the clothes when they are made.

This is all part of a more technical basis for what clothes should do and what we expect from them. We can call these things **performance factors**. A well-designed item of clothing satisfies both these performance factors (protection, lasting a reasonable period of time, etc.) and also **aesthetic factors** (fashion, social requirements, etc.). It has to do all this and still be at a **price** people can afford. How this happens in society today is the story of textiles.

bother people living in the tropics too much, but it is important for people in most parts of the world. This tells us that clothing has a little more to do than just be fashionable or make us look good. In the United Kingdom, for most of the time it is not a question of wearing clothes to be decent, but of wearing clothes to be warm enough or to keep out the rain.

Clothes then, have another job to do: to protect us. And not just from the weather. Workers in many industries have to wear special clothes to protect them from dangers at work. Think of people in a steel mill near a blast furnace, handling acid in a chemical factory, or fighting fires.

This tells us that the design of clothes may have to take into account far more than just appearance; it may have to offer protection as well. And not just protection, but the way the clothes perform generally. It's no use clothes looking good if they fall apart the first time we wear them – we often don't think about this when we buy clothes,

Summary

We all wear clothes, but the sort of clothes we wear and what they look like vary a lot and have changed a great deal through the centuries.

Our clothes depend on a mixture of **aesthetic** and social factors, and we are highly influenced by fashion. Even though we may know why fashions change, it is difficult to predict what will come next.

Clothes sometimes act as a uniform for a particular group of people, and they also have to meet certain **performance** standards. This can mean protecting people in dangerous situations.

Finally, all this has to be achieved at the right **price**.

Questions

1 Describe one item of clothing which might be socially acceptable in one culture but not in another.
Explain why one culture might accept this, but not another.

2 Discuss the points for and against the school rule: 'All lower school pupils must wear school uniform.'

3 Clothing can express your individuality.
a Describe two examples of this.
b What impression is each example you give trying to make on society?

4 Each of the following is used to try to express something to society. Suggest what that something might be in each case when worn by either men or women.
a pink hair
b a mini skirt
c a mink coat

5 Explain what you think is meant by the term 'fashionable'.

6 Discuss the feminists' view of women's fashion.

7 Describe the influence one particular person has made upon the fashion scene in the twentieth century.

8 Give four examples of special types of clothing needed for protection.

9 Discuss any properties you would expect your clothes to have so that they will perform as you would wish.

10 Explain briefly why each of the following factors is important when buying a textile item:
a aesthetics
b performance
c price

Design brief

1 As part of a United Nations International Year, design an outfit to be worn for school by boys or girls based on the traditional dress of a culture other than your own. The idea is to feature the style of the traditional clothing but adapt it to everyday school use.
What you must do:
a Decide on the traditional dress you are going to use. To do this you will need to look for pictures in books, magazines etc. Perhaps get ideas from somebody in your class who is from a different culture.
But remember, before you decide you must think whether the dress could be adapted to be a suitable school uniform.
b Think about the purpose of the school uniform. Is it just to make everybody dress the same, or is it meant to be noticed by other people, perhaps outside the school? Is it perhaps something that could be worn on other occasions?
c Adapt the traditional dress to the uniform, and draw and describe it, especially the changes you are making and why. If the dress is not a complete outfit discuss what you would need as well (e.g. if the traditional dress is a top, what it would be worn with, and in what style).
d If you have some experience of garment making discuss what kind of fabric and trimmings you might use and any special making-up methods. Think too about cost, how can you keep the price down so that everyone can afford it.

2 Select a sport and design a range of clothing to be worn as an after-sport outfit (like après-ski). It should be related to the sport but be suitable for social events rather than playing.

2
What are textiles?

2.1 Fibres at the base

We saw in Chapter 1 that clothes are part of our everyday lives – we'd be lost without them.

But how are they made? – From fabric, of course.

But what is fabric made from? – From yarns or threads.

And if you look closely at a piece of yarn (some knitting yarn perhaps), you will see it is made up of very fine hair-like materials – these are fibres. So, at the beginning, the whole process starts with fibres.

Let's look at this!
Fibre→Yarn→Fabric→Clothes

This simple chain of processes is the story of textiles. The fashion, the variety, the styles and the colours, all result from a few different fibres which are put together and made up in all sorts of ways. The whole chain then results in textiles. Within the world of industry, manufacturing is usually divided up into three parts. The production of fibre is the **Fibre Industry**, yarn and fabrics are the **Textile Industry**, and clothes are the **Clothing** or **Making-up Industry**. In this book we shall call the whole process textiles.

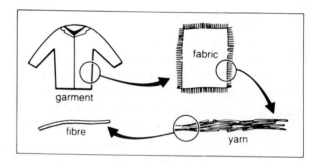

But let's start with the fibres.

▼ Actually, we could go further and say –
· what are fibres made from? The answer
· would be molecules, and particular types
· of molecules known as **polymers**, that is,
· molecules where the atoms of the
· different elements making them up are
· joined together in a long chain, rather
· like the shape of the fibres themselves.
· But, of course, in a single fibre there
· would be many millions of molecules.
· Each different fibre is made up of a
▲ different chemical compound.

Although all fibres are chemicals, where they come from varies. We usually divide them into two types: **natural** and **man-made**. Before 1900, only natural fibres were available, but since then man-made fibres have been used more and more, particularly since 1950. Here are some figures which show the use of fibres world-wide in 1960 and 1985.

Year	Total fibres used	Fibre usage – million tonnes							
		Cotton	Wool	Other natural fibres	Viscose	Polyester	Nylon	Acrylic	Other man-made fibres
1960	15	10	$1\frac{1}{2}$	1	2	*	$\frac{1}{2}$	*	*
1985	33	$14\frac{1}{2}$	$1\frac{1}{2}$	1	3	$6\frac{1}{2}$	3	2	$1\frac{1}{2}$

*negligible (very small) amounts

You can see two things – the big increase in the use of fibres and the rise in importance of the man-made fibres.

2.2 Natural fibres

Cotton We start with the world's most popular fibre – **cotton**. Although it is the most popular fibre world-wide, in the UK, Western Europe and America it has been overtaken by polyester, a man-made fibre. (Just think how much polyester/cotton fabric you see about.)

Although cotton is obtained by growing cotton plants, only part of the plant is actually the fibre. Cotton fibres are found attached to the seed in the cotton boll which develops from the flowers when they finally ripen or mature. The fibres have to be removed from the seed, and although years ago this used to have to be done by hand, it's now done mechanically by a process known as ginning. The seed is not wasted. Apart from those which are used to sow new cotton plants for the following year, the remainder are an important source of food, giving vegetable oils and a residue used for cattle feed. So for those countries that can grow cotton, it is a very important crop.

Cotton can be grown only where there is no chance of frost, so it cannot be grown in the UK or Northern Europe. Important cotton-growing areas in the world are the southern part of the United States, Brazil, India and China. Not only in these countries, but also throughout the world, cotton has been linked with important social and industrial changes, both good and bad, through the centuries.

▼   Cotton fibres are on average 2 to 3
· centimetres long. But there are several
· varieties. Sea Island cotton, mostly grown
· in the West Indies, is longer. American
· cotton is one of the most popular types,
· but this is not grown only in the United
· States, it is a species of cotton plant
· grown all over the world. Most of the
· cotton fibre is made up of a chemical
· compound known as **cellulose**. This is a

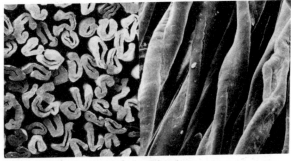
△ Cotton fibre magnified many times

· polymer found in all plants, but not
· always in the form of fibre. For example,
· cellulose is the main part of the whole
· cotton plant, but only when attached to
· the seed is the cellulose arranged in such
· a way that it can be used as a fibre.
· Cotton fibres when newly picked are
· round, but dry out after being separated
· from the seed and become a sort of
· twisted ribbon. However, they easily
· absorb water again and this property of
· cotton is one of the reasons why it is
▲ used for items such as towels.

Linen

Another vegetable fibre is **linen**. It was once popular but is now little used compared to other fibres. Linen comes from the flax plant but, unlike cotton, linen fibres are not attached to the seeds but are found in the stem. Linen is similar to cotton in many ways, but it tends to be rather stiffer and is more expensive to produce, and this has led to its steady fall in popularity.

▼   Because linen comes from a plant, it
· also, like cotton, is made mainly of
· cellulose. The difference is the way in
· which the molecules of cellulose are
· arranged. This different arrangement of
· molecules in linen makes it a different
· fibre to cotton.

· So we have already seen that to get a
· fibre we need a polymer and a way of
· getting that polymer into a fibre form. The
▲ cotton and flax plants do this naturally.

Animal fibres

Fibres can also come from animals. Our own hair is one example, but the hair of some animals has become widely used. The best known of these is, of course, **wool**.

Sheep live in most parts of the world except the tropics and very cold areas, but some varieties of sheep give better wool than others. The best variety is the Merino, and large flocks of Merino sheep are kept especially for production of wool in Australia. The average wool fibre is longer than cotton – about 10–15 centimetres – and the fineness of the fibre is often taken to be an indication of quality.

Because wool has been used for centuries, many names have come to be used to describe wool quality, often related to the places where those wools were first used. For example, Shetland wool means a fairly coarse type of wool often used for knitwear, but it doesn't necessarily mean that the wool came from Shetland. Botany wool is generally a finer quality, but the word Botany has no real meaning now, although it originally meant that the wool had been shipped from Botany Bay in Australia.

Although wool is very popular in the UK, in many parts of the world it is hardly used at all. That's why it comes low down in the league of world usage of fibres. Wool tends to be expensive, so for many people it is thought of as a luxury.

▼ Wool is a natural fibre, but it is a very
· different chemical compound from cotton.
· It is a polymer, but this time one known
· as a **protein** – a long chain made up of a
· number of simpler chemicals called
· amino acids. There are about 19 different
· amino acids in wool and the molecule is
· one of the most complicated known.
· Wool, like cottons, will absorb moisture,
· but it is of no use for towels because,
· when wet, wool fabrics tend to shrink
· badly. One of the features naturally
· present in the wool fibre is its crimp,
· and this means that when the fibres are

· made into yarn they can be very bulky,
· hence warm. This is why wool is often
· thought of as a warm fibre to wear; but
· now man-made fibres can copy the crimp
· in wool and give just as warm clothing
· and sometimes other advantages at a
▲ lower price.

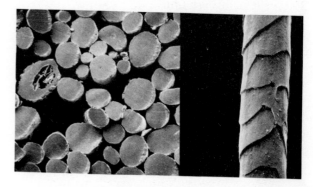

△ Wool fibre magnified many times

△ Two useful goats – Angoran (mohair), Kashmir (cashmere) and a rabbit (Angora)

There are other animal hairs used for clothes, especially knitwear. These include mohair, cashmere, alpaca and angora, and are all expensive.

So far, all the natural fibres we have talked about have been fairly short in length and certainly no use to be made up into fabric until they have been spun together to make a yarn. They are known as **staple** (i.e., short-length) fibres. But there is another natural fibre which is produced in a very different way, also by an animal but a very different animal from the sheep. This is **silk**, which is spun by the silk worm. The silk worm is part of the life cycle of a moth, which lays eggs that hatch out to give a caterpillar; this then feeds on mulberry leaves and grows until one day it spins a cocoon. It is this cocoon, made up of one continuous length of silk fibre, that the caterpillar remains inside until it changes into a moth. For centuries, people have taken these cocoons, killed off the caterpillar inside and unravelled the silk, thus producing one of the most beautiful of natural fibres, not this time in short lengths but in a continuous **filament**.

Silk produces beautiful shiny fabrics, but it is very difficult to wash, needs a lot of ironing, and is expensive, and these problems have limited its use. Most of the silk in the world comes from China or Japan.

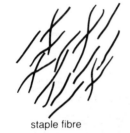

staple fibre   filament fibre

▼ Chemically, silk, like wool, is a protein
· but it is made up of different amino acids.
· This is one of the reasons why silk and
· wool are different. Another difference is
· the way the molecules are held together
· in the fibre and, of course, the way in
· which the fibre is produced. Wool is
· grown on the sheep. Silk is produced by
· the silk worm in its body as a liquid, then
· pumped through its spinnerets (or
· spinning organs) just like a spider
· spinning a web. It is this way of
· producing a fibre that is copied in all
· man-made fibres. We cannot copy the
· sheep or the cotton plant in the way they
· produce fibre, but we can and do copy
▲ the silk worm.

2.3 Man-made fibres

Cotton and linen come from plants, so when people began to think they might imitate nature and make fibres, the first place to start was with material from plants – the main substance from which all plants are made being, of course, cellulose. A plentiful source of cellulose was the wood from trees.

After many experiments, the first factory production of fibres from wood began in about 1900, and in the UK this developed into the company that is now the large textile group Courtaulds. The fibre produced was what today we call **viscose**, although it used to be called rayon.

▼ Viscose is made up entirely from
· cellulose which is the same as the
· cellulose in the wood. The difference is
· that, instead of the molecules being held
· together as they are in wood, they are
· rearranged to form fibres. For this
· reason, viscose is often called a
· **regenerated** fibre.
·   The process depends on dissolving
· wood in a pulped form in caustic soda
· (sodium hydroxide) and carbon
· disulphide. This produces a very thick
· (viscous) solution of cellulose. This
· viscous solution is then put through a
· **spinneret** (a metal disc with fine holes in
· it just like the rose on a watering can)
· which is immersed in a bath of sulphuric

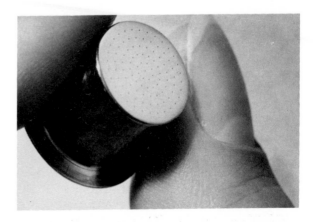

△ A spinneret

acid. The acid breaks up the solution of
cellulose, neutralizes the sodium
hydroxide, and viscose fibre is formed at
the spinneret. Because the fibre is spun
in sulphuric acid, the process is called
▲ **wet spinning**.

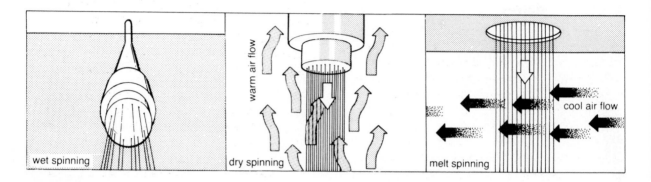

When spun, viscose is a continuous
filament, but it can be made into a staple
fibre simply by chopping it up. It is cheaper
than cotton but it is not as strong, especially
when wet; this is why you should never
wash viscose at high temperatures.

Viscose used to be very popular, and was
used for a great variety of things from
stockings to carpets, from coat linings to
blouses, but now it is much less popular.
Though still used for dresses and blouses, it
is now mainly used with polyester. An
improved viscose which is stronger and
more like cotton is now available, called
modal. It is often seen used with cotton in
underwear.

67% POLYESTER
33% VISCOSE

△ The common fate of viscose – junior partner of
polyester

▼ The problem with viscose, and why it is
weaker than cotton, is that when the
cellulose used to make it is dissolved, the
molecules are shortened, in other words,
they are broken. A polymer is a long

molecule made up of the same small
molecule (monomer) repeated over and
over again. Even breaking it does not
change its basic nature, but may, as
happens to the polymers in viscose,
▲ make it weaker when in a fibre.

Two other fibres have been made starting
from wood (cellulose). Chemical processes
are carried out on cellulose which change it
to give two new basic materials for fibres.
These are then spun to give **acetate** and
triacetate. They have different properties to
viscose and are used only as filament
yarns. Acetate looks rather like silk and it
used to be called artificial silk. But because
this could deceive people into believing
they were really buying silk, the use of this
term is now banned. Acetate and triacetate
are still used, mostly for women's wear, but
they are much less popular than they used
to be.

▼ The chemical process by which acetate
and triacetate are made is called
acetylation. It is simply carried out by
treating cellulose with acetic acid. When
the polymer is formed it is dissolved in a
different way to that used for viscose. An
organic solvent is used, which
evaporates very easily. The solution of

- polymer in the solvent is pumped through
- a spinneret into hot air, and this causes
- the solvent to evaporate very quickly at
- the holes of the spinneret and allows the
- fibre to form from the polymer which
- remains. This method is called **dry**
- **spinning**, in contrast to the method of
▲ spinning viscose.

So we have natural fibres and fibres made from a natural substance – wood. In the 1930s came a big breakthrough – the world's first **synthetic** fibre – **nylon**. Nylon was discovered in the USA by the giant chemical company Du Pont, and was part of a deliberate plan to design a substance which would make a suitable fibre for textiles. The basic raw materials were simple chemical substances obtained from oil, and these substances were built up **(synthesized)** to give a material which could be spun into nylon. (Although 'nylon' was the name originally given to this fibre, today it is often called **polyamide**.)

▼ The original method of producing nylon
- involved two chemicals, hexamethylene
- diamine and adipic acid, which joined
- together to form a nylon polymer. The
- way the atoms are arranged in the
- molecule gave rise to it being described
- as 'nylon 66'. This distinguishes it from a
- later method developed in Germany for
- making nylon using a simpler substance,
- caprolactam. This newer nylon is known
- as 'nylon 6'. Although to a chemist the
- nylons are slightly different, to the
- consumer they behave virtually
- identically in clothes, and you would
▲ never be able to tell them apart in wear.

Nylon (polyamide) was quite expensive when it was first produced, and very scarce, but from 1950 onwards it became widely available and very popular for clothes and household textiles as well as in industry. Since about 1975, its use in clothing and household goods has decreased, and it is now mainly used for stockings and tights, tough outer wear such as kagouls, and carpets. It is one of the world's strongest

fibres and is used very extensively in industry. Today, its price is less than cotton and wool but its place as an important synthetic fibre in clothing has been overtaken by **polyester**.

Polyester was discovered in the UK in 1941, but was developed only after World War II, by ICI in the UK. It is now made world-wide and is the second most important fibre in the world, with its use increasing all the time. It is synthesized from simple compounds obtained from oil.

▼ The final synthesis of polyester
- involves ethylene glycol and
- terephthalic acid. When the polymer has
- been made it is spun through a spinneret
- just like nylon, but both nylon and
- polyester are spun in different ways to
- viscose and acetate. They are simply

△ The silkworm (and the spider) copied as polyester is spun

- melted, and do not need any form of
- solvent and when the molten polymer is
- pumped through the spinneret it goes
- solid as it meets the cold air, forming the
- fibre. This is known as **melt spinning**.
- Polyester is used both as filament and
- staple fibre. Like nylon, polyester was
- expensive when first developed, but the
- price has gradually reduced until it is
▲ now cheaper than cotton or wool.

Another synthetic fibre developed in the 1950s is **acrylic**. This, too, is made from substances obtained from oil and was produced in an attempt to make a synthetic fibre which handled like wool but which had improved properties, particularly washability. Acrylic has been very successful. It is cheaper than wool and is used in staple form, particularly in knitwear.

A modification of acrylic, **modacrylic**, has the special property of being resistant to burning, and it is used for items such as dressing-gowns and pile rugs which might be used near a fire.

△ I'm safer with modacrylic – but I' be safer still if I didn't smoke

An up-and-coming fibre also made from oil is **polypropylene**. This fibre is not used much in clothing because it melts at a rather low temperature which would make it very difficult to iron, but it is used for carpets and furnishing fabrics as well as in ropes and for other industrial uses. It, too, is much cheaper than natural fibres.

△ Thank goodness we don't iron carpets!

Finally, mention must be made of a rather special fibre which has largely replaced rubber elastic for stretch garments. This is **elastane**, a very complicated substance, but again made from oil. It is expensive but has a tremendous amount of stretch (over 500 per cent), and it does not perish as rubber does when it is washed.

Fibre classification

We can summarize the sources of the different fibres like this:

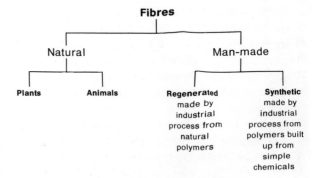

Blends

We have already said that cotton is the world's most important fibre, but that is not true for Western Europe and the United States. Polyester comes first, although cotton is close behind. The use of fibres is constantly changing with fashions and as new technical developments bring improvements to natural and man-made fibres alike. Of course, fibres are not used only on their own. Many of these are **blended**, that is, mixed together with each other.

I'm not perfect -but together we could **be** something..

LOVEMATCH..

Polyester

Wool

..OR MARRIAGE OF CONVENIENCE?

There is a very good reason for this. No fibre is perfect, none has all the properties that you would want. For example, we like the feel of wool but we would like to be able to wash it, we like the washability of polyester but we don't like the feel, so why not blend the two together and get the best of both worlds? Well, you may not get quite the best of both worlds, but you should get a sort of balance between the two which is better than the extremes of each one separately.

It is this idea that has led to the popularity of blends. Many of them use polyester, but the idea of blending began a long time before polyester was invented. One of the earliest blends was wool and cotton (the best known example of this has 55 per cent wool and 45 per cent cotton and is sold under the name Viyella).

Most of the blends work like this: people like the idea of wearing natural fibres, but they are expensive, and sometimes do not have the performance properties they would like, so man-made fibres are added and this brings the cost down and gives a better all-round performance.

Of course, it matters what percentage of each fibre is present. The fibre which has the biggest percentage is likely to be the one whose properties dominate the blend. For example, if you like the feel of wool it would be no good expecting it if there is only 10 per cent wool in the blend.

Most fabrics containing two or more fibres are blends, but occasionally the word 'mixture' is used. This applies when two or more different yarns (each containing different fibres) are used.

2.4 Labelling

When we buy clothes or any other textile items, we ought to know what they are made of. At the base, as we have seen, are fibres, and it's the fibres that are basically going to determine how the item performs. It is for this reason that there is now a legal requirement for all clothes and most other textile items when sold to have a label which tells the customer what they are made of and what percentage of each fibre is present.

▼ The regulation says a number of things:

· 1 All textile items must have a label
·   telling you what fibres are present. It
·   does not have to be sewn into the item
·   but it does have to be visible when
·   you buy it. If you don't see a label on
·   or near clothes that you are thinking
·   of buying, don't buy them. If a
·   manufacturer cannot be bothered to
·   keep within the law it is unlikely they'll
·   be bothered about other standards.

· 2 A label must tell you the percentage of
·   each fibre (unless it's less than 10 per
·   cent) and the most important fibre (the
·   one with the biggest percentage) must
·   come first. As an example, we have
·   the well-known blend 67%
·   polyester/33% cotton.

· 3 In garments with linings and other
·   important trimmings, these must be
▲   separately labelled.

One of the most important things about the labelling is that the common name for the fibre must be used (this is called the **generic** name). This was because when man-made fibres were developed the manufacturers used **brand (**or **trade)** names for these fibres rather than a common name, to try to make the public believe that their particular fibre was different and therefore better. Brand names, of course, are used for all sorts of things and not just textiles (think of baked beans or cornflakes). Sometimes the manufacturers use their own names, sometimes an invented name.

In textiles, polyester was sold under several different brand names – for example, Terylene (made by ICI in England) and Dacron (made by Du Pont in the USA). Acrylic was sold under brand names such as Acrilan (Monsanto, USA), Courtelle (Courtaulds, UK) and Orlon (Du Pont, USA). There was virtually no difference between the different makes of the same fibre, but many people believed there was, and to avoid this confusion the labelling regulations made it clear that the generic name had to be shown clearly. Manufacturers can add brand names if they want but these must not be more prominent than the generic name.

So don't get confused between the fibre and the brand name which may be used for it. Brand names usually have a capital letter at the beginning, a common or generic name should not.

Here is a list of the important fibres and some of the brand names you may see connected with them.

cotton

no special brand names but the fibre is promoted by the Cotton Institute using the cotton boll symbol

Pure Cotton

wool

no special brand names but promoted by the International Wool Secretariat (IWS) using the Woolmark label. This means the item is made from pure new wool and does not contain re-used (second-hand) wool

△ The Woolmark

polyester	Terylene, Crimplene, Dacron, Trevira, Diolen
nylon (now increasingly called **polyamide**)	Bri-nylon, Tactel, Antron
acrylic	Courtelle, Acrilan, Orlon
elastane	Lycra
triacetate	Tricel

Summary

Fibres are the basis of the clothes we wear and these are built up into yarns, then into fabrics and finally made up as clothes.

There are six really important fibres used for clothes; two are natural (cotton and wool) and four man-made (polyester, nylon, viscose and acrylic). There are several other, less important fibres. All fibres are made up of chemicals called polymers.

Fibres may be used on their own, but very often two or more fibres are used in blends.

All clothes must have a label showing the generic or common names of the fibres from which they are made, and their percentages. Brand names are also sometimes used, but these cannot be instead of the generic name.

_____ Questions _____

1 Are these statements true or false?
   a Wool is the world's most popular fibre.
   b All our clothes are made of polyester.
   c Blends contain different sorts of fibres mixed together.
   d Labelling on clothes should tell you the brand name of the fibre.
   e Polypropylene is used for all sorts of clothes.

2 Complete the following:
   a Acrilan and Orlon are brand names for _____ fibres.
   b The Textile Labelling Regulations say that garment labels must contain the _____ names of the fibre.
   c _____ fibre is especially popular for stretch garments.
   d _____ fibre is obtained from the Angoran goat.
   e _____ is a stronger form of viscose.

3 List as many fibres as possible that are used for clothes under the following headings:
   a Natural
   b Regenerated man-made
   c Synthetic man-made
   (Try to include some that are not mentioned in this chapter.)

4 a Why is cotton an important crop for the countries that can grow it?
   ▼
   ▲ b How could cotton be grown in the UK, and would it be worthwhile?

5 a What are blends and what are their advantages?
   b Name three blends commonly used for clothes.
   c What would be the main differences between the following blends:
      a 70% polyester, 30% cotton
      b 80% cotton, 20% polyester?

6 a What is the difference between staple and filament fibres?
   b Give a natural fibre example of each type.
   c Explain why man-made fibres can be made in both staple and filament forms.

7 Using the figures for world fibre use, construct pie charts for 1960 and 1985.

8 Explain the similarities and the differences between the following pairs of fibres:
   a Acrylic and modacrylic.
   b Viscose and modal.

9 Which of the following are brand names, and for what fibre?
   WOOL, TERYLENE, POLYESTER, NYLON, COURTELLE, LYCRA, POLYAMIDE, LINEN, MOHAIR, TACTEL.

10 What's wrong with the following
   ▼ garment labels?
   · a Wool/cotton
   · b Terylene/cotton
   · c 55% polyester, 25% wool, 10% nylon
   ·
   · d 30% wool, 70% acrylic
   ▲ e 100% polycotton

_____ Design brief _____

ICI have developed a new sort of nylon fibre which looks and feels like cotton, but is strong and washable like nylon and polyester. They have given it the brand name TACTEL.

They have offered a prize to the best design for clothes which can be used to advertise the new fibre.

Draw and describe your entry for the competition and write some slogans or words to go on the advertisement.

Idea: Look up a garment or textile item for which nylon used to be popular but is now thought of as old fashioned, and see whether the new fibre could improve on this.

3
How are textiles made?

Interesting though fibres may be, we cannot wear them just as they are; they have to be processed so that they will hold together and give us the sort of properties which we look for in a textile fabric. This fabric can then be made up into a garment. The invention of these processes goes back to pre-history, but today's industry uses the most modern technology. We begin by spinning a yarn.

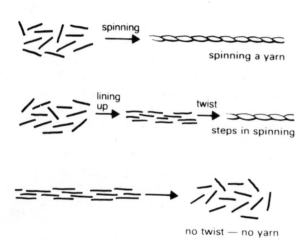

△ The web from the card is gathered to form a sliver, a thick but weak yarn

3.1 Spinning

We have seen that fibres come in two forms, **staple** and **filament**. Filament is already a long yarn so it does not *need* anything more done to it, although sometimes it is processed further, as we shall see.

But staple fibres are short and have to be made to hold together in a yarn. This is called **spinning**.

Spinning takes place in two main steps: lining up the fibres and then putting in **twist**.

Without the twist the yarn would fall apart.

We can see this at its simplest by looking at the traditional spinning wheel. The person using it lines up the fibres with their fingers and the turning of the wheel puts in the twist. Modern industry is a lot faster.

▼   In the first stages, called **carding**, the
·   fibres are lined up to form a continuous
·   sheet of fibres called a **web**. This web is
·   pulled together to give a thick rope of
·   fibres called a **sliver**.
·   Although a sliver is thick, it is weak,
·   and would easily pull apart, so it passes
·   through a further series of steps which

△ The final spinning stage where the twist is put in

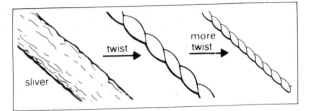

- draw it out to the thickness needed and
- put in twist, which holds it together. As
- twist is put in the sliver and it gets
- stronger, it also gets thinner (try it on a
- sliver made from some cotton 'wool'), so
- making a yarn is a carefully-worked-out
▲ balance of twist and thickness.

The development of machines to spin yarns from fibres was one of the first things to happen in the Industrial Revolution in the eighteenth century. In those days the important fibres were cotton, wool, linen and silk, particularly the first two. Whilst these are all fibres, their average lengths are different, so the machines that were invented had to cope with this. To do so, a different spinning **system** developed for each fibre. The basic steps in each system were the same (lining up the fibres and putting in twist) but the machine details were different. So there were systems for wool, for cotton, for linen and for silk.

▼ The wool and silk systems were a little
- more complicated. Silk is, of course, a
- filament so the silk spinning system
- (Schappe) included a process to break
- the filaments before spinning.
-   For wool, not one but two spinning
- systems were developed. Because of the
- natural crimp in wool fibres it was
- realized long ago that it could make bulky
- yarns for thick, and therefore warm,
- clothes and blankets. So the **woollen**
- spinning system developed to give high-
- bulk yarns with low twist. On the other
- hand, wool was needed for tough hard-
- wearing fabrics, so the **worsted** system
- developed with high twist and relatively
- low bulk.
-   Each fibre, therefore, had its own
- system, which could not be used for any
- other fibre. From the beginning of the
- twentieth century, however, the man-
- made fibres began to appear and as we
- have seen could be tailor-made to any
- length. This meant they could be adapted
- for use on any of the spinning systems –
- and they were!

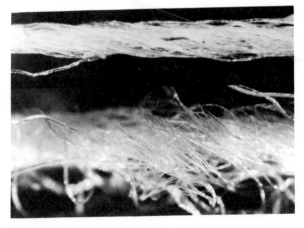

△ Yarn structure

Today, fibres like polyester are spun on all systems. This is especially important when fibres are blended together. Let's take the example of a popular fabric – 50% polyester, 50% cotton. Before spinning starts, equal amounts of polyester and cotton fibres are mixed together. Because cotton is present, the yarn has to be spun on the cotton system and so the polyester fibres have to be of the same average length as the cotton fibres. After mixing, spinning begins and the spinning process helps to mix the fibres more so that the yarn produced is ▲ an intimate blend of the two fibres.

Now, let's return to filament. Although it is already a yarn and could be used as it is, it is not right for every use. This is because it is thin (lacks bulk). There are some uses where thin, flat, shiny fabrics are required, and where the yarns must be packed tightly together (for example, parachute fabric or linings for garments) and flat filament (as it is called) is ideal. But what about others? How could we get bulk?

Filament could be chopped up to give short staple fibres and these could be spun in the usual way to give a bulky yarn, but this seems a waste of time (and money) when you have already got a yarn. Instead, we need a process to put bulk into filament yarn without having to cut it up. This is called **texturizing**.

It works like this.

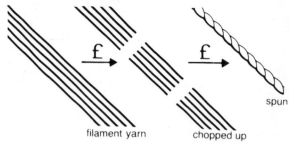

Look at an ordinary filament yarn. It is made up of a number of smaller filaments (monofilaments).

If each one of these could be crimped, it is easy to see how two things would change.

The yarn would be **bulkier**, and have **stretch**.

This is the basis of texturizing, which is used a great deal in the textile industry on polyester and nylon (polyamide). It produces a much cheaper yarn than ordinary spinning and the yarn is used for knitted (jersey) fabrics and wovens. You can always tell a textured yarn by looking at it under a magnifying glass – the crimped filaments are clearly visible.

There are several processes for texturizing yarn. All have two basic stages:

1 A way of putting crimp in the filaments.
2 Heat, which makes the crimps **set** (remain) in the filament.

Heat setting works best on polyester and nylon, hence their widespread use.

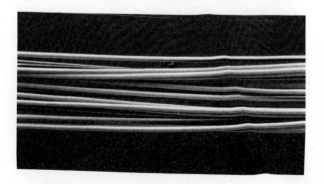

△ Flat filaments of man-made fibre

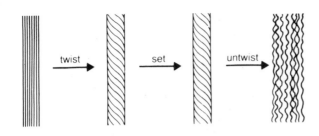

△ False twist texturizing

▼ By far the most important texturizing
· method is **false twist**. The spindle of the
· machine puts a lot of twist in the heated
· yarn in one direction, then the twist is
· allowed to unwind, but as it does so the
· yarn sets and the partly removed twist
· causes the filaments to crimp. This
· process is often carried out by the fibre
· manufacturer, and is very fast and cheap.
· It is used for nylon (polyamide) for stretch
· tights and for a whole variety of polyester
· fabrics (especially woven blouse and
· trouser fabrics and jersey).
  Another method which is becoming
· popular again is **air jet**. The heated yarn
· passes through jets of air which blow
· little loops and crimps into the filament.

· Because of the loops the yarn handles
· differently from false twist and has less
· stretch. An old trade name for this
· method was Taslan, and it is one of the
· methods used by ICI to produce
· polyamide yarn which handles like cotton
· and has the brand name Tactel.
·   Two other methods which have been
· used but which are now of little
· commercial interest are **stuffer-box** and
· **knife-edge**. In stuffer-box, the yarn is
· literally stuffed into a tube where it
· crimps and bends and retains this shape
· because of the heat when it is pulled out
· at the other end (trade name Ban-lon).
· Knife-edge works by the same principle
· that you use when you crimp your hair by
· pulling it over your fingernail. The heated
· yarn passes over a knife-edge which
· gives crimps and loops (trade name
▲ Agi-lon).

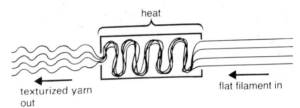

△ Stuffer-box

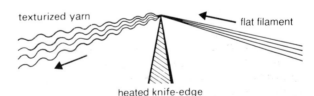

△ Knife-edge

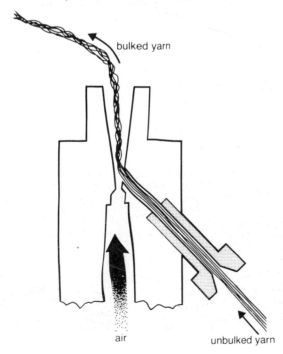

△ Air jet texturizing

When you are designing a fabric you need
to decide what yarn to use, and that means
not only what fibres are in it and how it is
made, but what size it is. The way size is
measured is based on the weight of the
yarn and is called the **count**. The weight or
count gives a good guide to thickness.

▼ The internationally agreed method is
· the **Tex** system. The count is defined as
· the weight in grams of one thousand
· metres of yarn. For everyday fabrics for
· clothing this gives rather low numbers, so

we usually use decitex (dtex), which is the weight of ten thousand metres.

Therefore, 160 dtex means that ten thousand metres weigh 160 grams, and a 100 dtex means the same length weighs 100 grams. So there is less fibre in the second yarn, and it will almost certainly be thinner or finer. Unfortunately, old habits die hard and people cling to their old systems. You may have heard of denier. This is an old system for measuring filament yarns and is the weight in grams of nine thousand metres. Once again, the smaller the number the finer the yarn.

But there are other systems which work the other way round, such as the cotton count (the old system used by the cotton industry). Here, the yarn is measured as the length for a fixed weight. A 40s cotton count means that there are forty 840-yard lengths in one pound of yarn. It works the other way to the dtex system because 60s would mean more yarn for the same weight, so that yarn would contain less fibre and so probably be thinner. These old systems do still survive – for example, on sewing threads.

The wool industry had its own system too, like cotton, but it was based on a different weight, and to make matters worse, worsted and woollen yarns were measured differently. Worsted was sized by the number of 560-yard lengths in one pound, and the Yorkshire woollen count (it was different in other parts of the country) was based on the number of 256-yard lengths in one pound.

Another important property of yarns is the amount of twist. Twist holds the yarn together and is measured by the number of turns (twists) per centimetre. Because you can twist a yarn either clockwise or anti-clockwise, the twist direction has to be known. It is either S or Z. This is important in building up more complicated yarns and in making fabrics. Yarn can untwist, and if balanced amounts of S and Z are not used the untwisting could cause distortion.

The yarn produced by spinning is one single thread. But added strength and improved properties can be obtained by twisting two or more single yarns together. This is what is meant by ply yarns, which you see on hand-knitting yarn labels. Two-ply means two single yarns twisted together, and so on.

But it can get even more complicated. Corded yarns are built up from a number of plied yarns. This happens occasionally for embroidery threads, for example, and other threads for decoration, but is far more important in industry where the method is used to build up very pliable but very strong ropes.

△ S and Z twist

△ Three singles twisted gives 3-ply

△ Two 2-ply yarns twisted gives 2-cord

Plied and corded yarns are generally made from yarns of the same fibre, but even more complex yarns are made by twisting different singles yarns together. The commonest example of this is **bouclé**, where 3 singles yarns are used, one forming small loops. Sometimes yarns are introduced which contain slubs in them or yarns are used to hold together sliver which is not very even and gives a slubby effect. By special spinning, little twists can be introduced, giving **knop** yarns.

bouclé yarn   knop (or knot) yarn

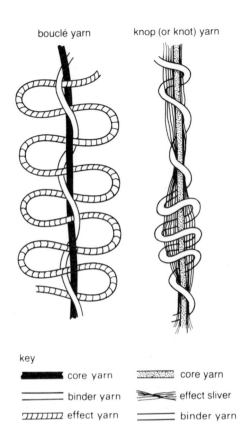

key

━━━━ core yarn

───── binder yarn

⊓⊓⊓⊓⊓ effect yarn

▧▧▧▧ core yarn

⟋⟍⟋⟍ effect sliver

═════ binder yarn

△ Bouclé and Knop

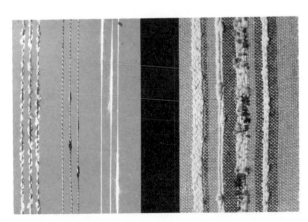

△ More special yarns and their uses

The story of yarns shows how design develops in textiles. We saw that the industry uses only about ten fibres, but the types of yarns available, in size and type, run into hundreds and that does not include all the variations possible using different colours. This opportunity to create new varieties becomes even greater as we look at fabric.

3.2 Weaving

Now we have a yarn, but that is not much use by itself, except, of course, the yarns designed and used as sewing threads and the small amounts used for decoration, such as embroidery.

The next step is to make a fabric.

△ Basic weaving

The problem is to find a way to make the yarns hold together but still keep the soft, flexible, draping properties we want in textiles.

Our remote ancestors found two ways of doing this – **weaving** and **knitting** – and these two methods have survived together. The main changes have been in how they are done – by hand on simple machines in the past and on the computer-controlled, high-speed looms and knitting machines of today.

Let's take weaving first. The fabric is formed by **interlacing** the yarns at right angles (90°) to each other. The friction between the yarns at the points where they cross holds the fabric together. If there is not enough friction between the yarns (if the fabric is not designed correctly) it will not hold together, leading to problems such as **slippage**, especially at seams. In all woven fabrics, the yarns at the edges will pull out fairly easily when cut – we call it **fraying** – and that is why when making up, the edges must be overedged, or joined with some other special seam.

△ It would be worse at a seam

So a woven fabric is made from yarns called **ends**, which run along the length of the fabric (this direction is the **warp**), and some called **picks**, which go across the fabric (this direction is known as the **weft**). At both edges along the length a special weave produces the **selvedge**, to stop fraying.

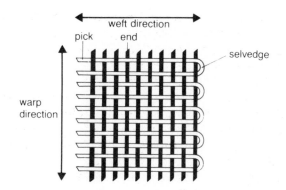

△ A woven fabric

▼ In the same way as we need a method to describe yarn size, so we need a method to describe the construction of the fabric, the way it is made. This is done by noting the number of ends or picks per centimetre (in some cases the old measure of per inch is used). So a fabric of 45 × 30 would have 45 ends (yarns) per centimetre in the warp and 30 ▲ picks (yarns) per centimetre in the weft.

One important piece of information we need to know about a woven fabric is the **pattern** in which the yarns are interlaced. The simplest of these is called **plain** weave: each yarn in either warp or weft passes over one, under one, and so on. When fabrics are being designed, this is represented on squared paper (it's a lot easier than drawing a woven fabric every time). A black square represents a weft yarn passing under, and a white one a weft yarn passing over.

A second very common weave is called a **twill**. The result of moving the position where the yarns pass over or under, and having the warp yarns pass over two weft

Plain weave and twill weave as done with graph ▽ paper

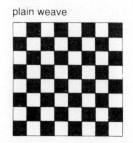

plain weave

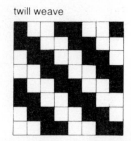

twill weave

yarns is to give a diagonal effect. Twills are very popular for trouserings because the structure is more rigid in the warp and hence slightly harder wearing.

The third basic weave is a **satin**, where the yarns pass over more than two yarns in the opposite direction. This **'floating'** of yarns on the surface can give a shiny effect.

But these are only three basic weaves. To this must be added **jacquard**, where the arrangement of over/under gives a complicated pattern, perhaps representing a flower or some other object; and finally, the weaves which can result in special raised or loop surface finishes such as **terry towelling**, **corduroy** and **velvet**.

Weaving offers the possibility of enormous variety. Think of all the different yarns and the many ways of arranging them in a whole variety of weave patterns and constructions. From hundreds of yarns we can get thousands of different fabrics – and there is still knitting to come.

▼ Now we can look at how weaving is
· carried out – on a **loom**. The basic
· problem is how to get the weft across the
· warp and at the same time arrange for
· the pattern.
· The old method uses a shuttle, as in a
· hand loom, but modern machines use
· other methods which are faster. In a
· loom, the warp yarns are first wound
· from a **creel** on to a **beam**. The beam is
· placed on the back of the loom and each
· warp yarn threaded through the eye of a
· metal wire called a **heald**, in two or more
· **shafts**. The shafts are lifted up and down,
· separating the warp threads to form an
· opening, or **shed**. The weft yarn is wound
· on to a small bobbin **(pirn)** and placed in
· a **shuttle**. The shuttle passes backwards
· and forwards through the opening. By
· controlling the way the warp yarns open,
· the weave pattern is produced.

△ A jacquard weave pattern

△ First stage – wind warp yarn on a beam

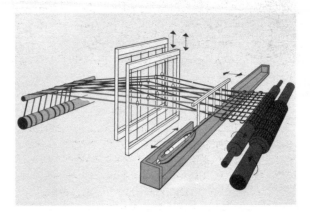

△ Basic loom weaving

- The ultimate in patterning is a jacquard loom in which every warp yarn is controlled individually to enable a complicated pattern to be produced.
- The first power looms, where the shuttle was knocked across the warp and back by the machine, revolutionized weaving when they were introduced during the Industrial Revolution at the end of the eighteenth century. They are still seen today, but have largely been replaced by faster (and quieter) machines which send the weft yarns across the warp in a different way. These are:

1. **Gripper** – the yarn is held by a small metal gripper which is fired across the warp like a bullet.
2. **Rapier** – a rod holding the yarn is thrust across the warp (like a sword thrust).
3. **Waterjet** – the weft yarn is fired across the warp in a high-powered jet of water (like a powerful water pistol).
4. **Airjet** – uses a jet of high-pressure air instead of water.

- Other things have also changed on looms. The control of the warp threads is now done by computers, so making it possible to change patterns very quickly if needed.

△ Jacquard loom – each string controls one warp yarn

One of the newer looms – waterjet ▷

3.3 **Knitting**

Now we can look at the second main way of
holding yarns together – knitting. The basic
principle is that we form **loops** and the
interlocking of these loops holds the fabric
together.

This can be shown by thinking about hand
knitting. The loops are formed (cast) on a
needle and by manipulation with the fingers
and another needle the yarn is fed in to
form another loop which joins the loop on
the needle. This can be done either with
one needle holding the yarn and one needle
being used to form the new loops, when
knitting a sweater, for example (straight
knitting), or in a circle using a number of
needles to hold the yarn, and one needle to
form the new loops as, for example, for
socks.

Now think of the way the yarn is fed in to
form the fabric. The fabric grows down-
wards and the yarn is fed in across the
fabric. To borrow a term from weaving – this
is in the weft direction; so hand knitting is a
form of **weft knitting**.

Weft knitting is very popular in industry as
well. Here, the needles used are rather
different from those used in hand knitting.
Each loop is held by a separate needle, and
industrial machines may be either **flatbed**
(straight) or **circular**. A scaled-down version
of a flatbed is sold as a knitting machine for
the home.

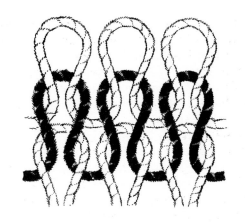

△ Basic knitting

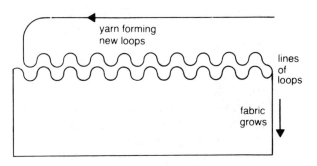

△ Why weft?

△ Flatbed knitting machine

△ Circular knitting machine

Flatbed machines produce a continuous length of fabric which can be cut up into shapes and sewn together to make garments. Knitted fabrics do not fray in the same way as woven fabrics do, although they may run; that is, the loops may be made to **unravel**.

A special type of flatbed machine (fully fashioned) allows loops to be cast on and off at the edges, as in hand knitting. This is used to produce sections of garments that are already shaped so that they do not need further cutting. Making up is therefore much simpler, and this type of garment is often referred to as **knitwear**. Many sweaters and cardigans are produced in industry in this way.

The circular machines used in industry have a variety of diameters. The smallest ones are used for making socks, stockings and tights. The larger ones produce the fabric as a tube which may be used as it is with a small amount of cutting (for example, for T-shirts), or it may be slit along the side and opened up, so making a flat fabric.

△ Fully fashioned pieces for a sweater

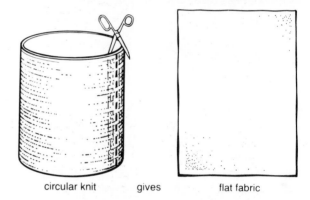

circular knit   gives   flat fabric

▼ Once again, we can see how a
· tremendous variety can be produced. But
· even more variety is possible when we
· think how patterns and different fabrics
· are created.
·   As the yarn is fed to each loop on a
· needle, the machine (or hand knitter) can
· either **knit** (i.e. form a stitch), **float** (not
· form a stitch) or **tuck** (hold a loop and let
· it take the next row as it comes along).
·   Because the term weft, borrowed from
· weaving, is used to describe the way in
· which the loops are formed, the loops in
· a knitted fabric are called by different
· names. The **wales** are the loops running
· down the fabric and the **courses** are the
· loops running across the fabric, so here
· again we can describe the construction of
· a knitted fabric in terms of wales and
· courses per centimetre. If we think of the
· stitches running in these two directions
· we can begin to see some of the different
· stitches which are used.

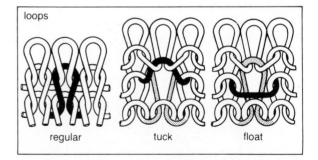

loops

regular   tuck   float

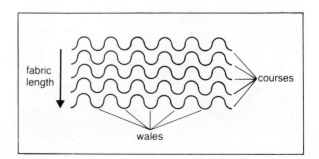

fabric length

courses

wales

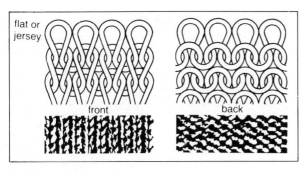

△ Flat or jersey

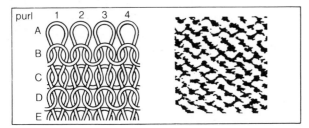

△ Purl knitting

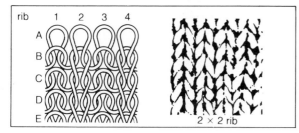

△ Rib knitting

△ A double jersey stitch

- In **flat** or **jersey** knitting, the loops are formed on one side of the fabric in both wales and courses.
- In **purl** stitches, however, the loops are formed on different sides (front and back) in alternate (every other) course.
- In **rib** stitch, the loops are formed on different sides of the fabric in alternate wales. If this is every other wale, it is known as 1 × 1 rib; 2 wales front, 2 wales back, 2 wales front and so on is 2 × 2 rib. Rib structures are highly stretchy and have good recovery from stretch, so they are used for cuffs and waistbands on knitwear or for garments which are tightly fitting on the body.
- If we think of all these stitches, the way loops can be formed and the fact that each needle can be controlled separately on a jacquard machine with different yarns being fed into a machine with hundreds of needles, the possible variety is enormous. And that's with just one set of needles. In **double jersey**, two sets of needles act together to knit two fabrics which are joined together in a kind of double thickness.
- Circular machines are very fast and are therefore a cheap method of fabric production, and with computer-controlled knitting, new designs can be drawn on the screen, programmed into the computer and fabric knitted in a matter of
▲ a few hours.

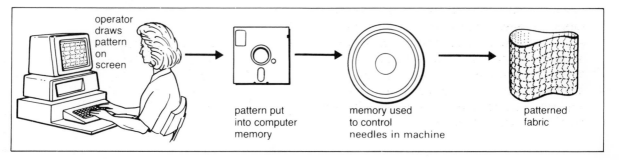

operator draws pattern on screen

pattern put into computer memory

memory used to control needles in machine

patterned fabric

Another method of knitting is **warp knitting**. This is different in that a separate yarn is fed to each needle, not one yarn across all needles as in weft knitting. This means the yarn is fed in the same direction as the fabric grows. The yarns are wound on to a beam (as in weaving) where each yarn passes through a guide before reaching the needle. Warp knitting is even faster than weft knitting and is the cheapest method of fabric production using yarns. A wide variety of patterns is possible and industrial machines have more than one set of needles and more than one guide bar, hence more than one yarn feeding to each needle.

But warp knitting machines have one big drawback: they work well only with filament yarn. That is why warp knitting is much less popular than weft knitting or weaving.

What are the main differences between knitted and woven fabrics which matter when you wear them? There are two, and both are due to the way they are made.

The yarns in a woven fabric are nearly straight, just a small amount of crimp as they pass over each other, and they can be packed tightly together. The loops are not straight in a knitted fabric and it is not easy to pack them tightly together. The results are:

1   A knitted fabric has much more stretch (weft knitted more so than warp knitted). Although woven fabrics have a little more stretch in the bias (diagonal), it is not as much as in the average knitted fabric. Stretch, of course, allows us to move with comfort. This is why knitted garments are preferred for close-fitting clothes like sweaters, underwear and tights.
2   Knitted fabrics are more porous. That is, they are more open so that air can pass through them more easily. Good on a hot day, not so good on a cold day.

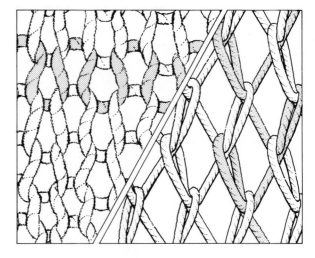

△ Weft and warp knitting – watch the direction the loops are formed

△ Just as well the fabric is knitted!

△ Come back woven fabric!

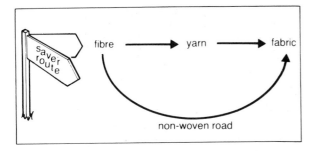

3.4 Non-wovens

The word non-woven could apply to knitted fabrics, but what is meant in industry is a sort of fabric not made by the traditional methods of weaving and knitting – the reason for this being to save money.

Traditionally, fabrics are made in two steps – fibre to yarn and yarn to fabric. If the yarn could be left out and we could go straight from fibre to fabric, money would be saved.

Let's go back to spinning. In the first stage, a web is made. Before it is pulled together to make a sliver it is a flat sheet like a fabric. If it could be made to hold together it would be usable as a fabric. This can be done in four ways:

1 Sticking – the web is covered with an adhesive (glue) which sticks the fibres together. This gives bonded-fibre fabrics, e.g. Vilene, commonly used as interlining. Making non-wovens by the adhesive method has some similarity to making paper, which uses cellulose from wood, and so items made from non-wovens are often called paper garments. This is not a true name, since a non-woven always starts by using a textile fibre, not just raw cellulose.
2 Punching – the web is punched with hundreds of hooked needles which make the fibres tangle together.
3 Stitching – the web is put under a series of sewing machines which put in lines of stitching to hold it together.
4 Fusing – the web is heated so that the fibres partly melt and then stick together.

Many fibres are used to make non-wovens, but the commonest are polyester, nylon (polyamide) and viscose.

Non-wovens are cheaper than wovens or knits, so why aren't they used for everything? The answer is that for many purposes they just cannot equal the properties which woven and knitted fabrics have and which we look for in textiles. For example:

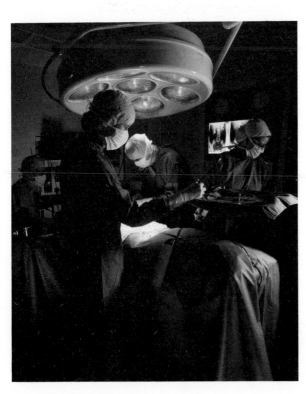

△ Looks don't matter here – so non-wovens win

△ No more non-woven trousers for me!

△ But they don't play on the curtains!

1 Most non-wovens are fairly (often very) stiff, have a firm feel and do not drape well – OK for interlinings but not for a main fabric.
2 They have poor strength, particularly resistance to rubbing. This is because there are no yarns so the fibres are not held in by twist, and so easily rub or pull out.
3 They have very little stretch.

Despite this, the cheapness of non-wovens has meant that they are increasingly used, and this works in two situations. First, any use where the inferior properties are less important, for example stitch bonded fabrics are used for curtains where abrasion does not matter. Second, **disposables** where the item is thrown away after a short time thus saving money on, for example, cleaning. An example is operating gowns in hospitals.

Gradually, paper and non-wovens and the disposable idea are making inroads into areas where traditional fabrics have been used. Some examples are: handkerchiefs, table napkins (serviettes), nappies, interlinings, pants, hospital gowns and filter bags.

△ Operating is a messy business and gowns need cleaning and sterilizing so it is cheaper to dispose of them

△ Two mucky ends but it's much easier to throw it away than wash it. But is it cheaper?

3.5 Finishing off

We may have made a fabric, but it is not ready for use yet – at the least it needs a clean and tidy up. But what is known as the **'finishing'** stage can be more than that. Various treatments can be carried out which change the **handle** (feel) and appearance or alter the way the fabric performs in use.

Let's look first at what nearly every fabric goes through – **cleaning** and **stentering**. These are part of what are sometimes called routine or general finishes.

After going through the factory the fabric may be dirty and have chemicals on it that were used in the processing, so that it needs cleaning. In this condition it is termed a **gray** or **greige** fabric. Usually, cleaning involves washing (water and detergent – called **scouring** in the trade), but sometimes the fabric is dry cleaned. After washing, when the fabric is wet, creased and even a bit **skewed** (out of shape), this is where stentering (or tentering) comes in.

In the stentering process, the fabric is held flat by each selvedge between clips or on pins. If you have ever noticed down the selvedge of a fabric a line of pin marks, that is where it has come from. These used to be seen on all fabrics, but are now less common as clips are used because they do less damage to delicate fabrics. The fabric, on its clips or pins, moves through an oven which dries the fabric and sets it in a flat form free of creases. The chains which hold the pins or clips can be moved to help pull the fabric into shape.

▼ There are many other finishes which can be applied to fabrics. Those which alter its properties are sometimes called **functional** finishes, and may be simply mechanical or involve the use of chemicals. All are done as a continuous process, but remember, the more finishes, the higher the cost, so a lot of finishing will be carried out only on fabrics which can sell at a good price, for example wool worsted suiting. Here, first of all, are some of the mechanical finishes and what they do.

1 **Calendering (pressing)**. This changes the surface appearance of the fabric by pressing it between heated rollers or plates. If a design, such as fine lines or a definite pattern, is cut on the rollers, special surface effects like **moiré** or **embossing** are produced.

△ A stenter

△ Pin marks from a stenter

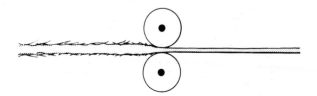

△ Heated rollers

△ Moiré fabric

· 2 **Brushing**. The fabric is passed
·   through a large rotating brush and this
·   is one of the processes used for
·   raising the surface of a fabric, for
·   example in winceyette. Sometimes
·   after brushing the fabric is **sheared**
·   (put under a knife blade rather like a
·   large lawnmower blade) to produce an
·   even surface.

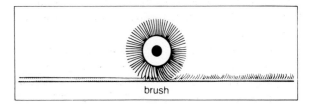

brush

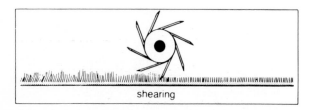

shearing

· 3 **Crabbing**, **decating** and **fulling**. These
·   are three special processes using hot
·   and cold water and sometimes steam,
·   which are applied to wool fabrics to
▲   produce a soft full handle.

Many finishes involve chemical
treatments which greatly change the way
fabric behaves, or guard against a possible
problem in use. Here are some of the
important ones.

1 **Resin treatment**. One of the most
   important of these uses polymers
   applied to cotton and viscose fabric. This
   changes these materials from fabrics
   which need a lot of ironing after washing
   and which dry slowly to fabrics which
   need little or no ironing and dry quickly.
   (That's how you get easy-care cotton.)
   There is a problem, however, in that the
   finish reduces the strength of the fabric,
   and for this reason the treatment has
   become much less popular in recent
   years.

2 **Washable wool**. The big problem with
   wool – that it shrinks **(felts)** when
   washed – has been overcome by a
   special finish applied to the surface of
   the wool fibre. This is sold under the
   name **Superwash**, and is applied
   especially to wool knitwear. It makes
   wool garments fully machine washable.

3 **Flame retardant finishes**. The best
   known of these is Proban, which greatly
   reduces the fire risk with cotton and
   viscose fabrics. But there are problems:
   some of the finishes are affected by
   washing, some cause fabric to be stiff,
   and some may themselves be poisonous
   (toxic).

4 **Waterproofing**. Fabrics may be coated
   with a plastic material (polyvinyl
   chloride or polyurethane) which makes
   them completely waterproof. This is the
   method used today, in place of the old
   treatment, which used rubber. The so-
   called waxed cotton garments are
   usually made like this. Finishes can also
   be applied which, although not making
   the fabric completely waterproof, do
   reduce the risk of rain seeping through.
   These finishes (usually silicones) are
   called showerproof, but are less popular
   than they used to be, not because we
   have less rain but because some in the
   past were of such poor quality that
   customers became suspicious of any
   claims made for them.

▼ 5   Mothproofing. Protein fibres such as
wool and silk are attacked by moths
and carpet beetles. Actually, it is the
larvae or caterpillars of the moth that
attack the fibres, after the moth has
laid eggs in it. Mothproofing is
particularly applied to carpets,
because the chemicals tend to be
removed by washing and so are not
very suitable for clothes.

6   Mercerization. The oldest known
chemical finishing, but now very little
used. Caustic soda is added to cotton,
and this makes it swell. The result is
that the fabric is a little stronger, can
be dyed more easily and has a
brighter, shinier appearance (lustre).
This finish is used on some cotton
sewing thread (Sylko).

There are numerous other chemical
finishes, including anti-static, anti-soil
▲ and anti-bacteria.

At the end of the finishing process the
fabric, having been cleaned and
straightened on the stenter, is rolled up or
folded neatly ready for the next stage –
making up into the clothes we wear or an
item we can use.

Summary

Textile items are made in a series of steps.
Staple fibres are spun to give yarns,
which may be woven or knitted to make
fabrics.
Filament fibres may be used as they are
or given bulk and stretch by texturizing. The
most important texturizing process is called
false twist.
Weaving is based on interlacing yarns
and, by changing the way this happens,
different weave patterns, such as plain and
twill, can be made. Great changes have
taken place in the way the weft is laid
across the warp; the old shuttle has been
largely replaced by faster methods such as
water- and air-jets.
Knitting is based on loops which are

locked together. The most popular form at
present, like hand knitting, is weft but there
is another type, known as warp. Some
knitting machines are straight (flat), bed, but
the fastest are circular.
Non-wovens are a cheap way of making
fabric because by this method fibres are
turned into fabrics without making a yarn.
Some are used for clothes, but they do not
have all the properties of woven or knitted
fabrics and so are not satisfactory for every
sort of item.
Even when a fabric has been made, it still
needs finishing. Some finishes are quite
simple, some alter the surface or look of the
fabric, and some chemical finishes can
greatly change the way the fabric performs.

Questions

1   Are these statements true or false?
 a Spinning means putting crimp into
    fibres to give bulky yarns.
 b Nylon and polyester filament yarns
    are often texturized.
 c Woven fabrics usually have more
    stretch than knitted ones.
 d Warp knitting is carried out on a
    loom.
 e Jacquard looms can make highly
    patterned fabrics.
 f Easy-care cotton is weaker than
    cotton which has not had a resin
    treatment.

2   Complete the following:
▼ a _____ is the first stage of spinning
    which helps to line up the fibres.
 b Woollen and _____ are spinning
    systems originally developed for
▲   wool fibres.
 c _____ is used to dry and straighten
    fabrics during finishing.

3   a What are the two main differences
    between woven and knitted fabrics?
 b Explain the reason for this.
 c How do these differences affect the
    choice of fabric for the clothes you
    wear?

4 a What is a woven fabric?
▼ b How is it made?
· c How has the production of woven
· fabric been speeded up in the last
▲ 50 years?

5 a List three methods for getting bulk
▼ of texture into filament fibres.
· b What are the basic principles behind
· these methods?
· c Why is texturized yarn cheaper than
▲ spun yarn from staple fibres?

6 a What fibres are these finishes used
for?
(i) Superwash
(ii) Easy-care resin
b Describe in what way the finishes
change the properties of the fibres.

7 a Give three methods of making non-
woven fabrics.
b How do non-woven fabrics usually
differ from woven fabrics?
c Why does this make non-woven
fabrics generally unacceptable for
everyday clothes?

8 Discuss the similarities and differences
between weft, warp and hand knitting.

9 The following are textile items:

▼ staple fibres, filament fibres (or yarn),
· spun yarn, fabric, texturized yarn.

· These are processes:

· spinning, weaving, texturizing,
· finishing, knitting, warp knitting, weft
· knitting.

· Match the items to the processes, e.g.
· spinning – staple fibres (NB there may
▲ be more than one answer).

10 a List four spinning systems, including
▼ two for wool.
· b Why can polyester fibre be used on
· all four systems while cotton
▲ cannot?

Design brief

1 In industry the various stages in
producing fabric from fibre, e.g.
spinning, are usually carried out in
different factories, often belonging to
different companies. Many people
believe that it is more efficient to
complete all the stages in one big
factory; fibre would go in at one end and
finished fabric would come out at the
other.

You have the opportunity to set up a
factory like this, and you have to prepare
a report on what you would put in it.

Your task is to decide on two fabrics
which you think are very important in
textiles, for clothes or household goods,
and which if you made them on a large
scale would sell all over the world. For
the first part of your answer, list your
two chosen fabrics and explain why you
think they are important and will sell.
▼ The description of the fabric must be
· complete – for example, 50/50
▲ wool/cotton spun yarn woven.

The next stage of the brief is to outline
the various production stages that you
would put in your factory – for example,
whether you want spinning or
texturizing, and the order in which they
would go. You must also include means
of colouring or decorating the fabrics so
that they can meet the fashion
requirements of the market you have
chosen. Try to give as much detail of the
various stages as you can.
▼ Try to explain why you have chosen
· one process instead of another – for
· example, why you have chosen spinning
· instead of texturizing, perhaps. Is it for
· aesthetic reasons, or perhaps economic
· reasons?

Finally, list other things you would
· need to provide in your factory – for
· example, services such as electricity
· and water, and draw a plan of your
· factory showing not only where the main
· production processes would go but also
▲ where some of the services could be put.

4

How are clothes made?

4.1 Patterns

We now have the possibility of a whole range of fabrics, but usually we can't wear them exactly as they are. There are a few cases where this can be done, such as the Indian sari, which consists of a length of fabric cleverly wound and draped around the body; but most clothes have to face the problem that fabric is flat while human beings have a shape which bulges and curves at various places.

So how do we get from a flat fabric to a garment on a human being? How do we get the shape we want? Mostly, this is done by cutting the fabric into various pieces which when joined together give a garment that fits. The size and shape of the individual pieces are all part of the design of the final product, the garment. So let's look at that first stage – the **pattern**.

Before we begin, any pattern has to fit the person it is designed for – in other words, we have to know the right size.

When you buy clothes ready made they are sold based on certain standard **size charts** which have been built up over the years as giving the right body measurements for a large percentage of people. All these size charts should now be given with metric measurements, but the change over to metric is going very slowly in the UK, and it looks likely that for many years to come we shall see both inches and centimetres used. The conversion between the two is not helped by the fact that the number of centimetres in an inch is not an exact number, but 2.54.

For women's wear, the old size system of 10, 12, 14, 16, 18, etc. is still used. This relates to definite bust, waist, and hip measurements as shown in the table.

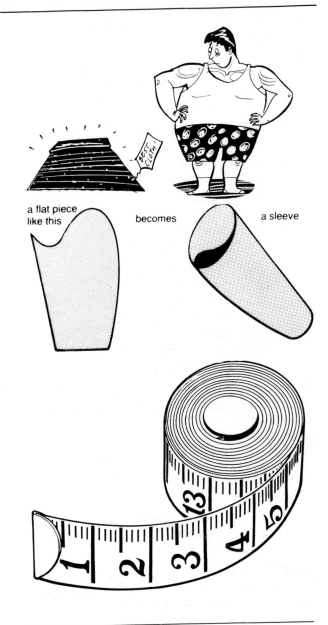

a flat piece like this   becomes   a sleeve

Size		10	12	14	16	18
Bust	cm	81	86	91	97	102
	in	32	34	36	38	40
Waist	cm	56	61	66	71	76
	in	22	24	26	28	30
Hips	cm	86	91	97	102	107
	in	34	36	38	40	42

For men's wear, garments are based on chest, waist and inside leg measurements. For shirts, the collar size is used. Trousers are usually sold based on waist and inside leg, with more than one inside leg length for each waist size, but sometimes they are sold with a leg which has not been completely finished, leaving the customer to finish it off at the bottom to the exact length required.

Children's wear used to be based on age, but that does not work very well because children of the same age can be very different in size. However, children of the same height usually have similar body measurements, so the recommended way of sizing children's clothes is to use height together with an approximate age, and the height is related to definite chest and other measurements.

The sizes described above are those you need to know if you are buying clothes in a shop, but you will need to know much more than that if you are a designer in a factory or a dressmaker at home.

Designers in factories also work to standard size charts, but these have a lot more measurements on them than the simpler ones which people use when buying clothes. People who make clothes for particular individuals (bespoke tailors, dressmakers etc.) take the exact measurements of the people concerned and make a special pattern for them. This, of course, is not really necessary if you are of average build and average proportion, but if you are different from the so-called standard size – very tall perhaps, or rather short – then you may find it difficult to get a good fit from ready-to-wear clothes. For clothes which give a good fit you may have to go to a special tailor, or make your own (although there are shops which cater for the so-called 'outsize').

▼ Let's assume we have got all the measurements right; how do we make a pattern? Remember that the pattern doesn't only have to fit, it has to include the shape and style features that are wanted, to meet current fashion perhaps. This not only means the outline shape, but also details such as pockets, lapels or trouser bottoms.

In a factory, each size of a particular garment will have a standard **block pattern**, and the pattern cutter will take this standard block and adapt it to give the style and fashion details required, as well as any variation in size. So part of the final pattern will include what is often called 'ease', which is the alteration of the basic size to allow for the shape and style of the garment – whether it is loose, baggy fashion or close, body-hugging fashion. When the pattern has been prepared, it will probably be tested by making it up in a simple, plain fabric and fitting it on a model, either human or dummy.

At home, dressmakers will buy a pattern from one of the many firms which specialize in them, such as Simplicity, Vogue or Butterick. If they are skilled, they may modify that pattern to suit their, or their friend's, individual shape, and the pattern may contain more than one **'view'**, that is, it may be adaptable to more than one style of garment. But whichever way you do it, you finish up with a set of patterns, and these are laid ▲ on the fabric ready for cutting.

But how does a pattern manage to produce the shape that is needed for a garment? Let's look at two basic garments – tops and trousers – and show how shape is built up through a pattern.

In a top, jacket or blouse, there is an opening at the front and the garment will have two foreparts, left and right, and one or two backs. Each sleeve is in one piece and is inserted at the shoulder (inset sleeve). One method of getting extra shape on the body is to use **darts** (V-shaped pleats in the fabric). These are common at the bust and chest area, and sometimes at the waist. Not all sleeves are inset; some are joined into the body fabric in a different way, reaching right to the neck of the garment – this is a raglan sleeve.

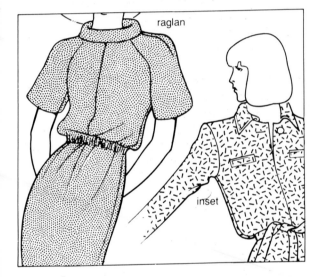

△ Sleeves

Attached to the top may be pockets, which can be either patch or in a seam – that is, inside the garment and entered through a seam which is part of the construction or cut deliberately for the purpose.

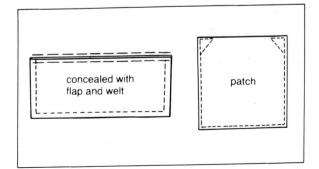

△ Pockets

The top may have a collar, and here there is a great variety of styles; the collar may also extend down through a lapel.

The sleeves may be short or long. If they are long, they will undoubtedly finish in a cuff – here again, there are many varieties.

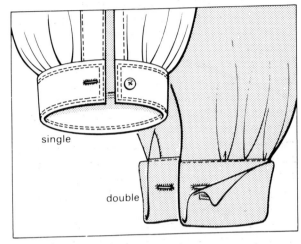

△ Cuffs

The opening at the front will generally require some way of closing it. Most garments are single breasted, but some are double breasted – that is, the fronts overlap. The most common closing methods are buttons and buttonholes, press-studs or zips, but there are other, more decorative (and expensive) methods.

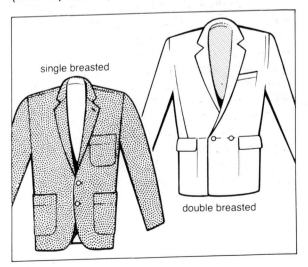

In the lower area, trousers are the most common garment for men, although both trousers and skirts are, of course, worn by women. Trousers come in a variety of styles: pants, jeans, culottes, bermudas etc. Usually, they require four main pieces of fabric (two for each leg) plus a waist band. The pieces are joined along the inside and the outside of the leg, and from the front to the back through the legs (crotch seam). Again, they may have pockets – sometimes patch, sometimes inset through a seam, and sometimes both. Although some have elasticated waists and no opening, especially those for children, most have some sort of opening, either at the front or at the side, which is usually closed with a zip.

▼ A pattern is not made just to fit a particular size and to make a particular style, it also has to take into account the sort of fabric that is going to be used. We have already seen in Chapter 1 that clothes need to look good and to perform to the standard that is expected, and that applies to everyday clothes just as much as to industrial clothes. Here are some examples of how the fabric and style can affect the pattern.

1 If the garment has a lot of making-up details on it, for example pleats, pockets, seams etc., it would be foolish to use a fabric with a bold pattern which could be broken up and distorted by all the making-up detail, or might hide the making-up detail so that it would have been a waste of time doing it.

2 If a garment is to be used for outer wear and a tough waterproof fabric is to be used, things like pockets and collars need to be designed to keep out the rain and not act as points where rain could get in, thereby ruining the purpose of the waterproof fabric.

3 Some styles need stiff fabric to give them the best appearance, while others need soft, draping fabric for the best effect.

4 Finally, always remember that the more making-up detail there is, the more time (and in factory production, therefore money) it takes, which means that the garment will cost more at the end. Too much detail may simply price the garment out of the market.

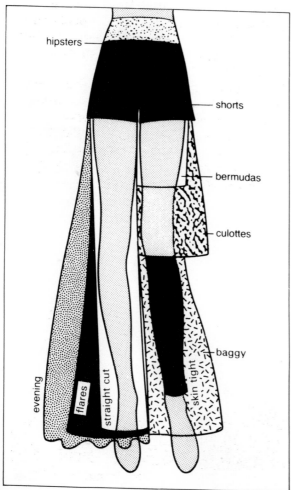

△ Trouser styles – fashions old and new

4.2 Trimmings

Although the main fabric is the most important, a garment consists of more than just that. It contains other fabrics and accessories known as **trimmings** (haberdashery in dressmaking).

Perhaps the most important trimming is the **sewing thread**, which is used to join the pieces of fabric together, and sometimes for decoration. Most sewing threads now are made from polyester. This has taken over from cotton because it is stronger and in particular does not rot, for example from perspiration. There is no reason why polyester thread cannot be used on any fabrics, natural or man-made, but 100% polyester threads, made from filament yarn, do cause a problem when machine sewing because of the heat produced in the needle. They may melt, thus giving a break. Two types of thread are sold which overcome this problem. In the first, the polyester filament is covered with cotton (core spun), and in the other, staple polyester fibre is used and spun like any staple yarn.

Sewing thread manufacturers sell their thread using brand names which tend to alter. For the home dressmaker, the main brands are Coats Drima (spun polyester), English Sewings Sylko (cotton), Super Sylko (spun polyester) and Gutermanns (spun polyester).

The size of sewing thread, of course, has to be right – the thicker it is, the stronger, in general, but there is no point in using too strong a thread, which might be unsightly. Sewing thread manufacturers use count systems for indicating the size of their threads. On the systems they use, the smaller the number, the thicker the thread – 40s or its equivalent is used for sewing heavier fabrics as well as buttons and buttonholes, and 50s or 60s or their equivalents for lighter-weight fabrics.

While the sewing thread is the most important trimming, because every garment has it, the **lining** may be the biggest, or nearly so, because the lining in a fully-lined coat can use almost as much material as the main fabric.

The lining hides the seams and the inside of the fabric, thus improving the look of the garment. It also makes the garment easier to get on and off, especially in the sleeves, but it must match up to the performance of the main fabric if it is going to give satisfactory use. Most linings today are of woven polyester or nylon (polyamide) filament, although in the past viscose and acetate were used. In the UK we put only a small amount of lining in trousers, but in the rest of Europe it is common to line trousers down to the knees. Skirts may be lined or unlined. A lining is often used to prevent a loosely woven outer fabric from bagging or slipping at the seams.

An important type of lining is pocketing, and this needs to be strong and hard wearing. The old sort of cotton pocketing was really not good enough. Most pockets are now made from polyester or nylon (polyamide) fabrics.

Linings usually need to be smooth and shiny, which is why they are made from filament yarns (the most expensive traditional lining is made from silk). But woven filament fabrics do tend to fray easily, and it is important that linings are finished correctly to prevent this.

△ The cost of a weak pocket

Although soft, flowing lines are often what we admire in textiles, there are some parts of garments that we want to be stiff, perhaps to make a collar stand up or to help a front to keep its shape. In this case, the trimming used in called an **interlining**. Older interlinings, particularly those for suits, were often called canvasses and were made with heavy yarns, including some containing horse hair. But today nearly all interlinings are made from non-woven fabrics which can give just the right degree of stiffness. Sometimes interlinings are sewn into the garment, but usually they are fused. To do this, a non-woven interlining fabric is coated with a plastic material which melts under heat. It is then placed against the main fabric and a heated press or iron is used to fuse the two together. This method is now used for shirt collars and fronts of jackets, as well as for making belts and, using double-sided fusible fabric, even for fixing hems.

There are many other trimmings that are used, such as tapes and bindings. These give stability to the garment. For example, tape can be used on the shoulder seams of knitted garments to prevent the fabric from stretching.

Shoulder pads are often made of fibre, although some are foam.

Many different types of trimmings are used in connection with fastening, both for tops and bottoms. These fastenings not only have a job to do in holding the garment together, but are very often used as a fashion or style feature.

Buttons are the oldest form of fastening. They come in a great variety of forms:

Without shanks – these have two or four holes, and are the sort most usually used in industry because they can be sewn on with button-sewing machinery.

With shanks – generally more expensive and used on outer garments.

Covered – these are specially made and covered with the same fabric or one that contrasts with the main garment. Covered buttons need to be tested carefully, because

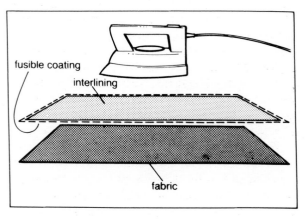

△ Fusing a fusible interlining

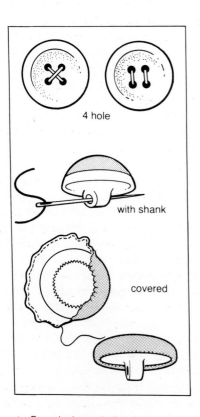

△ Four hole and shank buttons

many of them do not stand up to washing.

Zips have taken over from buttons and buttonholes in many outer garments – in trousers and in anoraks, as well as in a whole variety of sportswear. They all work in the same way: some form of 'teeth' fixed on tapes are made to join together by the action of a slider. The first zips had metal teeth, and these are still used but, because they are not so decorative, metal zips are usually concealed, for example in a skirt. For lighter-weight garments, polyester or nylon teeth are satisfactory, and generally less visible. These are also used for so-called 'invisible' zips, where the teeth are completely hidden when the zip is closed. For big decorative effects, zips with large plastic teeth, often in bright colours, are used. Zips, of course, come in any length to suit the garment, may be closed at the end or open ended (for jackets), or may be curved to fit on trousers and jeans.

Press studs are another form of fastening. These are usually made of metal although sometimes plastic is used. They need a special machine to fit them into the garment. Press studs are sometimes used together with a zip for garments that are worn in severe outdoor conditions. One of the problems with zips is that rain can penetrate the teeth, and so on storm-proof anoraks the zip fastener is covered with a guard which is then fastened down with press studs.

Two other types of fastening are popular with dressmakers, although not used as much in industry. Hooks and eyes are a very simple form of attachment, but are fiddly and because they have to be attached by hand are too expensive for mass-produced garments. Touch and close tape (best known trade name Velcro) is also popular with dressmakers because it is easy to fix. It consists of two tapes of nylon specially made so that one has hundreds of little loops and the other hundreds of little hooks; when pressed together, the hooks link up with the loops to form a fastening. The problems of touch and close tape are that in long lengths it is difficult to line up,

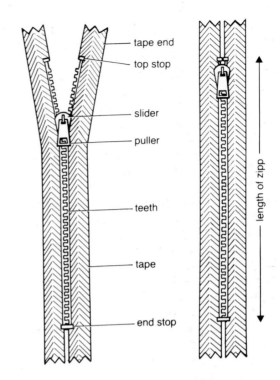

△ Zips

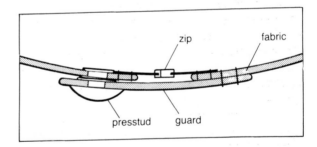

△ Stormguard from above

that it makes quite a noise when being opened, which can be a bit embarrassing in public, and that when it is opened the little hooks and loops tend to pick up dirt and dust which finally stop the tapes from operating properly.

4.3 Making up

So now we come back to cutting out. Having selected our fabric and trimmings we are at last ready to lay the pattern on the fabric and begin. But it is still not quite as easy as that. The pattern has to be laid on the fabric in the right direction, and we have to lay the

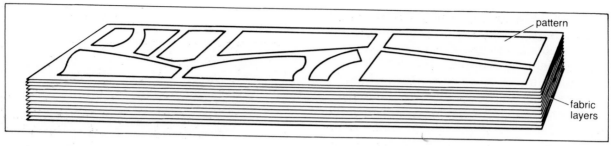

△ Garment lay

pattern in such a way that we use as little fabric as possible (unless, of course, we don't care about money).

If the fabric has a nap or pile, like corduroy, then we have to make sure that all the pieces are facing in the same direction and that we will not get pieces side by side in the garment where the pile is running in different directions. If the fabric is made up of stripes or checks in a bold design, we may want to arrange the pattern so that these match up when the pieces are joined together. Finally, we want to be as economical as possible.

In industry, that last factor is very important, because even a few centimetres saved per garment by carefully laying the pattern can mean a great deal of money when thousands of garments are being made. So in industry, **lay planning**, as it is called, is a vital part of the making-up process.

Factory-made garments are very seldom cut out just one at a time. The fabric is laid up in many layers, one on top of the other, and then the pattern is placed on top of all the layers and made to fit so that the minimum of fabric is wasted. Only when that has been done will cutting begin. A pair of shears or scissors would be suitable for cutting only one or two layers of fabric, and even for home dressmaking electric scissors are available which speed up the process. In industry, only a bespoke tailor would probably still use shears. With many layers of fabric, a factory uses an electric knife, cutting through perhaps a hundred layers at once.

Another method used in industry is **die cutting**. Knives shaped exactly like the part to be cut are laid on the fabric and then pressed through with a heavy press (a bit like a pastry cutter). This gives a very accurate cut and when used on a large scale is highly economical.

When all the pieces are cut, they then have to be joined together in the correct way. The method of joining almost always used is the sewing machine. Various ways of fusing together fabrics have been tried and are used on a small scale in industry, but sewing remains by far the most popular method. The problem is holding the pieces in the right position while the seam is being made.

In home dressmaking, this may be done with pins or by **basting** (tacking) the parts together with cotton thread. Basting is also used to a limited extent in bespoke tailoring. These processes are too expensive for mass-produced clothing, however. Instead, pieces are held together by the skill of machinists, or by using a special attachment on the machine.

Before joining the pieces together, one other sewing operation may be necessary. Woven fabrics tend to fray, and unless the edges are sealed in some way to prevent this the fraying will cause the seam to disintegrate later in the life of the garment. The usual method of doing this is to use **overedge** stitch (often called overlock in industry). This stitch usually involves three threads, one being a needle thread, although in some sections of the trade a two-thread overedge (serging) is used. This is the first sewing operation on many garments, and machines are available which can handle some shapes without needing a machinist.

In home dressmaking, overedge machines are generally not available, and other methods have to be used. Pinking for garments which are going to have to be washed is virtually useless, so the best methods are to run a zig-zag stitch along the fabric, to use one of the seams which conceal the edges of the fabric, thus preventing fraying, or to bind the edges of the seams.

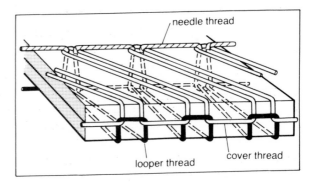

△ Three thread overedge stitch

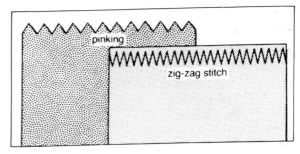

△ Poor alternatives to overedging

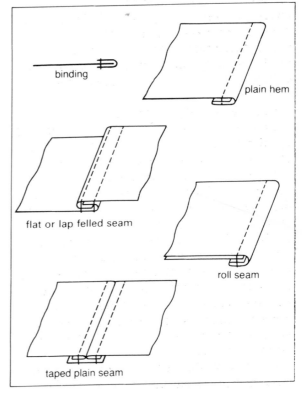

△ Good but expensive alternatives to overedging

A plain pressed open seam is the usual way of making the join in both industry and home dressmaking. In industry, the joining seam and overedging are sometimes combined in one operation (known as overedge safety stitch), or sometimes an overedged seam is used to join two pieces of fabric. The latter is especially used for knitted fabrics.

Except on expensive garments, complex seams such as French, lapped, run and fell, piped or corded are not used in industry. The reason, as you may guess, is that they take too long and therefore cost too much.

The most popular stitch used for general seams in both industry and in home dressmaking is the lock stitch. This is the type of stitch made by the standard sewing machine. Of course, in industry, sewing machines run at much faster speeds than they do for domestic purposes. An average domestic machine may be capable of 500 stitches per minute, while the average industrial machine does over 5,000 – so you can see how skilled an industrial machinist has to be.

▼ In using a lock-stitch machine there are several points to be noted to get the best results:

1 The correct number of stitches per centimetre should be used; too few and the seam will gape and be weak, too many and the fabric may be damaged to the point where it may be seriously weakened. A good average is 5–6 stitches per centimetre, and this should certainly be kept to if seams are to be elastic enough for use with knitted fabrics. If the seam does not 'give' when the knitted fabric is stretched, it may break. That is why an overedge stitch is sometimes used for seaming on very stretchy knitted fabrics (for example, on tights), because this type of stitch has more stretch.

2 The seam should always be made with the correct tension balance. If not, the stitches will be weak because threads

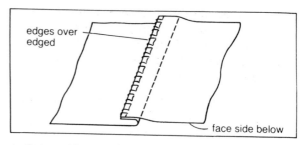

△ Belt and braces – overedge safety stitch

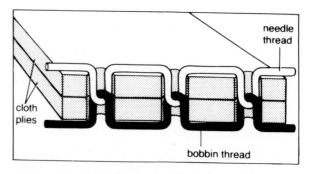

△ The standard lock-stitch machine

△ The fabric is willing but the seam is not

- will not be in the centre of the seam
- as shown in the diagram. Also, they
- will have reduced stretch, which
- may make them weaker when knitted
- fabrics are used.

- **3** The finest needle possible should be
- used, otherwise fine fabrics may be
- damaged. Size 10 or 11 is about right
- for fine fabrics (continental 70–75),
- going up to a maximum of size 18
- (continental 110) for the heaviest
- fabrics. For most purposes, a sharp-
- point needle is best, but there is a
- slight advantage for knitted fabrics in
- using a ball or rounded point.

- **4** The feeding mechanism should be the
- finest possible that will transport the
- fabric through the machine. If the feed
- mechanism, in particular the teeth, is
- too heavy, it may feed the fabric
- unevenly, giving unsightly results.

- **5** If the tension on the threads is too
- high, puckering or gathering can take
- place at the seam. If the bobbin case
- tension is kept to the lowest possible
- which will give a satisfactory stitch,
- adjusting the top thread tension to
- give a balanced stitch will give a
- satisfactory result overall. Too many
- machinists tighten up the tension
- when they get problems, and this is
- ▲ usually the wrong thing to do.

For sewing stretch fabrics at home, a zig-zag, which is a kind of staggered lock stitch, is best. Most domestic machines will do this stitch by simple adjustment.

▼ In industry, the lock stitch, although the
· most popular stitch, does have a rival in
· the chain stitch. The advantage of chain
· stitch machines, although they use a little
· more thread, is that they do not have an
· underbobbin, and this means that the
· machine does not have to be stopped
· frequently to load a new underbobbin.
· The saving of time for machinists doing
· long seams is well worth the slight
▲ amount of extra thread used.

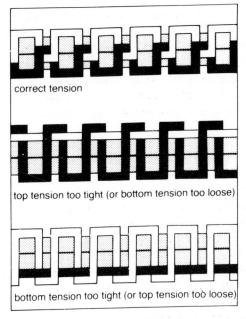

correct tension

top tension too tight (or bottom tension too loose)

bottom tension too tight (or top tension too loose)

△ Balancing act

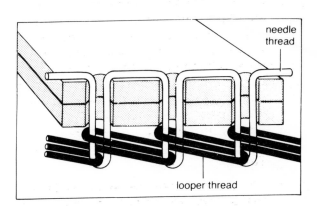

needle thread

looper thread

△ Two thread chain-stitch

The final seam to be done is often the fastening of the hem. This may be done with a lock-stitch seam, but more often than not you do not want to see a seam around a hem, or you may want a seam which can be easily unravelled so that it can be altered at a future date. There are several hand-stitch variations for hemming. The common machine stitch used in industry is called a blind stitch, and this is done by a special machine with a curved needle.

4.4 Pressing

Once the garment has been joined together (made up) it needs to be pressed and made ready for sending out to the customer. In fact, in both industry and home dressmaking, pressing may be done along the way to help keep the garment in good shape as it is being made. This is called underpressing, and in expensive tailored garments it is a very important part of the process of getting the garment into the right shape to fit the customer. However, the final press is the most important. At home, dressmakers may use a domestic iron, but in industry much heavier presses using steam are employed.

With an iron, we cannot simply use any temperature we like – the correct temperature has to be chosen to make sure that the fabric is not damaged. Domestic irons have three settings, 1 being the lowest. The table shows the symbols used on labels, the maximum temperature on the surface of the iron and the number recommended for particular fabrics.

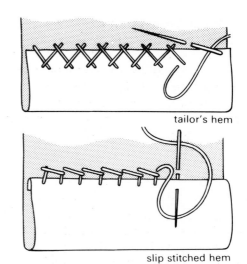

tailor's hem

slip stitched hem

△ Handstitched hems

△ Industrial steam iron

HOT (200°C)   WARM (150°C)   COOL (110°C)   DO NOT IRON

1 Cool – silk, acetate, acrylic, triacetate, modacrylic, polyester, nylon
2 Warm – easy-care cotton, wool, polyester/cotton blends
3 Cotton, linen, viscose, modal

Steam irons often have another setting which is used when steam is required.

How is the temperature controlled in an iron? The iron contains a thermostat which controls the supply of electricity to the heating plate of the iron, switching on when the iron is too cool and off when it has reached the required temperature (like the controls in a domestic oven).

But here lies a weakness. If the thermostat is faulty the current may not switch off when the set temperature is reached, and the iron may overheat. So you may think you are on the cool setting when you are actually on hot, so damaging a delicate fabric. When you are ironing delicate fabrics always be careful in case you have a faulty iron.

1 Never start ironing until the light which indicates that the iron is heating up has switched off.
2 Always start on a part of the garment which, if it were damaged, would be less conspicuous.

Irons are used in industry, although they are often steam only and heavier than the average domestic type. But in addition, special presses are used. These are quicker because they can cover a bigger area at a time. The commonest is a steam press often called a Hoffman press, which is for general use. For some purposes, presses specially shaped to fit different parts of garments are used. A simple version of these types of presses has been produced for domestic use, but most people do not have the space for one.

▼The basic Hoffman press works like
· this:

△ Hoffman steam press

· 1 The item to be pressed is placed on
·   the bottom buck, making sure that it is
·   not creased (or, if it is, that the crease
·   or pleat is wanted on the garment).
· 2 The top buck is lowered and steam
·   passed through the item from the top
·   and bottom.

· **3** The top buck is now clamped tightly to
· the bottom buck (to give pressure).
· **4** The top buck is released and the
· vacuum applied to the bottom buck;
· this sucks air through the item,
▲ removing the steam and cooling it.

Presses are used not only to press out creases, but also to put in pleats in, for example, trousers. For pleated skirts where many pleats are required, a press would be too slow because the pleats would have to be pinned or tacked into place first. Two methods are used to make such pleats:

1 *Formers* – card is folded to the shape of the pleats and the fabric is placed between two of these and bound together with string.

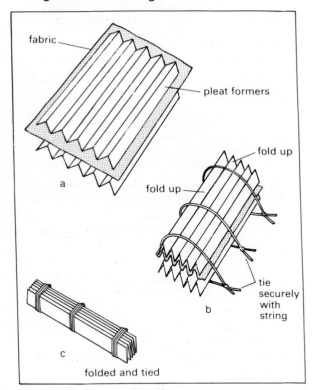

△ Pleat formers

2 *Pleating machine* – the pleats are formed by machine and the fabric length wound on to a roll.

To set the pleats, the formers or rolled fabric are steamed under pressure in an oven.

Pleats have names which relate to their type:

accordion	sunray if flared, crystal if small
knife	
box	

Although the garment may look finished in the factory when it is pressed, there still remains the problem of getting it to the customer without creasing or damage. Larger garments are generally put on hangers, perhaps covered with some sort of bag and transported on racks in specially constructed lorries. Garments travelling long distances are stored on hangers in containers which are carried on ships or aeroplanes. It is a specialized business to transport garments so that they arrive at their destination – the shop – without having to be re-pressed.

Smaller garments are not transported in this way. They are folded and put in bags or boxes. Sometimes this presentation, as it is called, can be quite elaborate – as, for example, with men's shirts. If you have ever unpacked a shirt you will know just how many pins, cards and stiffeners there are – and there always seems to be a pin left over when you put it on.

_____ Summary _____

Making up converts the flat fabric into a garment. First, a pattern is needed and this has to ensure the right fit and include all the style and fashion features.

Most garments have a main fabric and a number of trimmings. The most important trimming is probably the sewing thread, but there may also be lining, inter-lining, zips, buttons etc.

Garments are virtually all made up by sewing. There are several types of stitch, the commonest for main seams being lock stitch. Overedging is important; it is used to stop woven fabrics from fraying, and sometimes as a seam for knitted items.

After making up, garments are pressed using irons or, in industry, special steam presses, to make them ready for sending on to the retailer or distributor and then on to the customer.

_____ Questions _____

1   Are these statements true or false?
   a   A garment pattern is always made to give a skin-tight fit.
   b   A Hoffman press is used for die cutting fabric.
▼ c   Puckering is caused by low tensions on the sewing machine.
· d   Chain stitch is often used in industry instead of lock stitch.
▲

2   Complete the following:
   a   _____, not age, is the best basis for size charts for children.
   b   Polyester and _____ have largely replaced _____ and acetate as garment linings.
   c   _____ fabrics are the commonest interlinings.
   d   Woven fabrics tend to fray so they are usually _____ before seaming.
   e   The temperature of an iron is controlled by a _____.
   f   _____ pleats are small accordion pleats.
   g   Industry uses a _____ steam press for finishing garments.

3   a   Name three types of stitch commonly used to make up garments.
   b   What is each specially used for?

4   What methods could you use to make
▼ sure that seams in knitting garments
▲ have enough stretch?

5   a   Name three methods of closing the front on a jacket or top.
   b   Compare these methods for use on a school anorak.

6   a   How would you put a pleat (crease) in a pair of trousers, in the home and in industry?
▼ b   Compare the two methods and
·   explain why the industrial method is
▲   likely to be faster.

7   The following are textile items:
▼ polyester/cotton core-spun yarn,
· filament nylon woven fabric, adhesive
· bonded fibre non-woven, woven
· polyester tape, mercerized cotton
· sewing thread, polyester/cotton woven
· fabric, woven wool fabric.

· The following are garment trimmings or
· parts:

· bodylining, jacket front interlining,
· buttonholes, sweater shoulder seam,
· trouser pocketing, trouser leg seam.

· Match the items to the trimmings or
· parts, e.g. bodylining – filament nylon
· woven fabric (NB you may not need all
▲ the items).

_____ Design brief _____

Select an old (clean!) garment. Sketch it, noting all the main features. Then, starting with the seams, take it apart and find out how it is made.
   Here is some of the information you can find:
   a   types and number of seams
   b   trimmings – linings, pocketing etc.
   c   number and shape of main fabric pieces.
   d   how the main fabric and trimmings are made – woven? knitted?
   e   type of yarns used – spun? filament?
   f   fibres.
▼   Then, starting with the fibres, draw a
· flow diagram showing how the garment
· was made. (You should have several
· starting points all coming together in the
▲ finished garment.)

5
Where else are textiles used?

You can imagine what it would be like if we had no clothes, but can you imagine what it would be like if we had no textiles at all in the world? The soft, draping qualities of textiles, combined with their strength, have more uses in the home than you imagine, and there is a tremendous variety of uses for industry and in work and play outside the home.

5.1 Home uses

Just think how many items in each room of a house are made of textiles, and the list rapidly adds up. Remember, too, that many of the things we use in the home are also used in offices, shops, hotels, restaurants etc.

First, there is what is often called **household 'linen'**. The name comes from the fact that years ago most of the items were made from linen fibre, although, of course, that is no longer true. Included in this are bedclothes, and design has changed here a great deal. We used to have sheets, blankets and pillowcases. Now, most of us have **duvets** (continental quilts)

with a cover and sheets and pillowcases, blankets having largely disappeared, although you still find them in hotels. The duvet itself is made of textile fibres. It has a woven fabric cover and the inside is very often filled with fibre **'batt'** – just loose fibres held together with an adhesive. Some are filled with feathers and although these are warm, they are not washable like the ones filled with textile fibres. Even mattresses have textile fabric covers, and may include textile fibres as part of the padding inside.

One item which used to be common in the home but is now much less seen is a table cloth, and the fabric napkins or serviettes that went with it are now often paper. But curtains are still used everywhere, in all sorts of fabrics from heavy, thick velvet to light, printed cotton and not forgetting net, which is a knitted textile (usually polyester). Curtains are often lined. There is a number of reasons for this. Lining makes the whole curtain thicker, which makes it a better insulator, keeping heat in the home. It also protects the main fabric from sunlight which weakens the fabric and can cause dyes to

▽ A section through an average bed

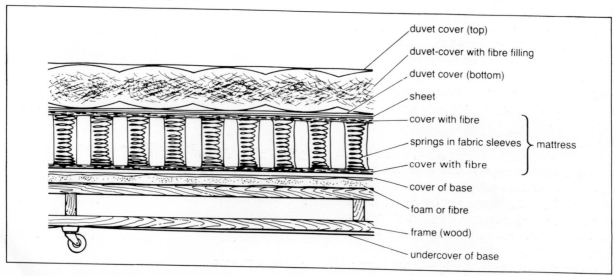

duvet cover (top)
duvet-cover with fibre filling
duvet cover (bottom)
sheet
cover with fibre
springs in fabric sleeves } mattress
cover with fibre
cover of base
foam or fibre
frame (wood)
undercover of base

fade. Yet another reason is that it just looks nicer, because the lining conceals the seams which may be joining the curtain fabric inside. Nowadays, special linings are sold which have an additional coating which reflects heat back into the room; these are part of the drive to save fuel. Once again, you can see that the reason for items being made from textiles is made up of a combination of things; partly necessity (curtains should keep us private), partly to look good (appearance) and partly for a definite performance reason (warmth).

But there are many more textiles in the home. Chairs are very likely to be covered with some sort of fabric, and these covers may be fixed, or perhaps loose, so that they can be easily taken off and cleaned. Then there are the towels we use for drying ourselves, and for drying the dishes, and dusters for cleaning the house. Even the simple duster is specially designed for its purpose – the brushed surface makes the dust stick to it more easily, and not fall off until we shake it.

While paper has taken over some of the traditional textile uses, textiles are now used for some of the traditional paper uses. For example, we see more and more textile fabrics used as wall coverings.

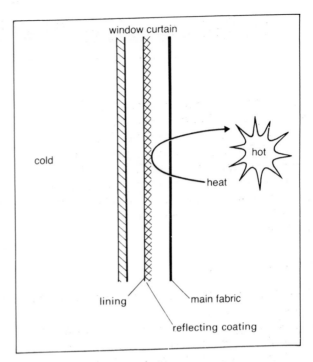

△ Curtains designed to help save energy

5.2 Carpets

Of all the textile uses in the home, the largest amount of fibre is probably found in the carpet, together with any rugs which may go with it. In the past, carpets were available only to very wealthy people, but since World War II new methods of carpet production have made carpets much cheaper, and therefore available to more and more people.

A carpet consists of two parts: a **pile**, that is, the fibres which are on the surface; and a **backing**, which really holds the surface pile together and stops it falling out. On some carpets there is an additional part, an **underlay**, often made of foam which is stuck to the backing.

The traditional sort of carpet was made by

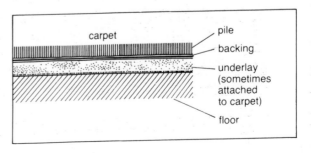

△ The basic carpet

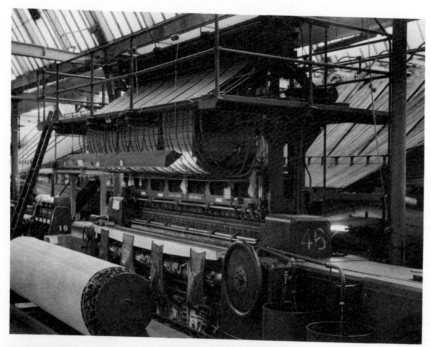

◁ Carpet weaving –
the Axminster way

△ Hand weaving Indian carpets

weaving the pile and the backing at one time. The backing was usually made of a fibre called **jute** which, like cotton, comes from a plant, but is much stiffer and harsher. Not the sort of thing you would want to wear as clothes, but very satisfactory for the tough life as the backing of a carpet. On many carpets today jute has been replaced by the man-made fibre polypropylene. On traditional woven carpets, the pile was wool but today, although wool is still the most important fibre in this area, it is often blended with nylon to give extra strength.

The two main types of traditional woven carpet are **Wilton** and **Axminster**; both named after the places where they originated, but now made world-wide. The weaving on both is very complicated and slow, so these carpets are expensive. Wilton carpets are usually plain, but Axminsters have a variety of patterns because it is easier to form a pattern with Axminster weave. Wilton carpets are the hardest wearing of all, but they are also the most expensive. Of course, in some parts of the world, carpets and rugs are still woven by hand. These often use wool, and sometimes exotic fibres like silk; they include carpets from Persia (the old name for Iran), India, Afghanistan etc. The skills are still there, but the cost goes up all the time.

The most widely used carpets are those which resulted from the new carpet-making technique which made carpet available more cheaply. Here, the backing is woven separately and the pile is then put into the backing as **tufts**, using a special machine. If you have ever made carpets or rugs using thrums (short lengths of wool which are pushed into a backing and then tied into a knot), it is a similar sort of process, except that the tufts are not held in by tying a knot, but by an adhesive which goes on to the backing. The backing in tufted carpets may be jute or polypropylene, and the pile can be a variety of fibres, sometimes wool but also nylon, acrylic, polyester and polypropylene. Viscose was used for a while, but it is weak and so gave poor performance in carpets.

Another new method of carpet making is now becoming popular – **flocking**. Here, the backing is produced separately once again. It may use woven or non-woven fabrics, which are coated with adhesive and the fibres are then dropped loosely on to the surface. Sometimes they lie partially flat and give a sort of matted appearance, but sometimes they are made to stand upright by putting a static charge on the backing which attracts one end of the fibre. Carpets made this way can have the fibres very tightly packed together, which means that dirt and dust do not easily penetrate, and this type is particularly popular for kitchen carpets because it also resists liquids seeping through. (An example of this type of carpet is Flotex.)

The traditional way of making carpet may have given way to other methods, but for floor covering, textiles in the form of carpets are more and more popular.

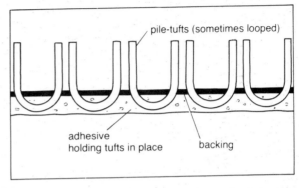

△ Tufted carpet – the revolution that made carpets cheaper for all

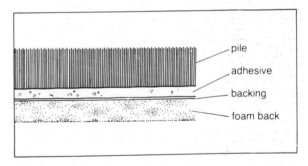

△ Flocked carpet – the tightly packed upright pile keeps dirt and liquids out

5.3 **Industry**

Textiles are not just used in the home. They are also used throughout industry for a variety of purposes. Of course, offices and shops have curtains and carpets, but the many different properties of textiles mean that they are used much more widely than that. Here are some examples of other uses.

1 **Coated fabrics**. Plastics are used a lot in industry (as well as in the home), but plastic sheet tears easily. To overcome this problem, a fabric (usually woven, but sometimes knitted) is used as a base and coated with plastic. This gives the plastic strength, but keeps it flexible. Enormous amounts of coated fabrics are used for tarpaulins (on lorries, railway wagons etc.), and they are also used for the skirts of hovercrafts, escape chutes and, nearer home, for plastic covers for furniture and for coats (imitation leather).

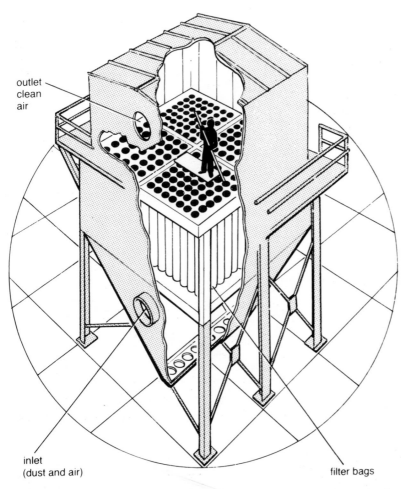

outlet
clean
air

inlet
(dust and air)

filter bags

△ Industrial filtration – if you don't believe how
much fabric is used look at the size of the man
and the number of bags

2 Filters. This may not sound very glamorous, but in many industrial processes solids need to be removed from liquids or gases. A textile fabric can be made just open enough to let the liquid or gas through while keeping the solid behind; such a fabric will be tough and flexible. Nearer home, your vacuum cleaner may have a textile fabric doing the same sort of filtering job.

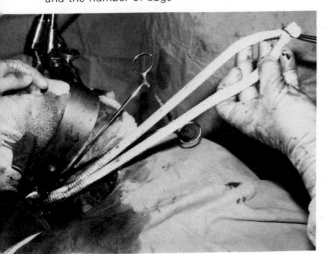

△ Replacement artery – no textiles – no blood – no
life

3 Hoses and tubes. The long hoses that fire brigades use need to be flexible enough to roll up neatly, but also tough enough to stand up to wear and tear. Most of these are made from polyester, which is tough but dries quickly after use.

A very different type are the knitted tubes made especially for use as artificial arteries in humans.

4 Conveyor belts. Again flexible and tough, a woven textile is supple enough to go round the corners at the end of a conveyor belt yet still strong enough to carry a heavy load from one place to another.

5.4 Ropes, cord and string

How would we manage without these things?

– parcels couldn't be tied up
– ships could not be moored to the dock
– mountaineering would be very dangerous
– clothes could not be hung out to dry

If you think about it, we might make do – sticky tape, metal chains or wooden rails are all answers to the above list – but ropes, cord or string provide a better answer in most cases. Again, there is a combination of flexibility and toughness with relatively light weight (compare a metal chain with a rope).

Ropes, cord and string are all made from textile fibres, previously cotton, **manila** and **hemp** (all plant fibres) but now mostly nylon, polyester and polypropylene. The man-made synthetic fibres are stronger, more resistant to rotting and lighter; polypropylene is light enough to float – quite useful if you drop a boat rope overboard by accident. They are also cheaper – natural fibres come in short lengths which have to be spun into a yarn, while synthetic fibres can be produced as a continuous filament so that this stage of processing is not necessary. Of course, a rope is not just one filament, but is made up of many filaments plied (twisted) and corded together. This builds up strength, but keeps flexibility.

In addition, don't forget that cord forms the basis of all types of nets – from tennis to fishing.

5.5 Tyres

If we think of tyres, we think of cars (not to mention lorries), and immediately we see more textile uses here – most vehicle seats are now covered with fabrics, from plushy velour to the firmer cord. Seat belts are also made of textiles (usually polyester), flexible enough to roll up or fold away but strong enough to hold firm in the case of accident. But there are still more fibres elsewhere in the car, and from a safety point of view these are even more important than the seat belts – those in the tyres.

Modern tyres are an important part of the whole design of a car. They have to transfer the power of the car to the road to make it move, and then stop it safely when necessary, and they must withstand road conditions (wet or dry, rough or smooth), help keep the car stable on the road, and last a reasonable time. Natural or synthetic rubbers can do some of these things, but they just do not have the strength and flexibility needed; so tyres are made stronger by the use of textiles. A tyre is built around yarns. The names for the two basic types of tyres – **'cross ply'** and **'radial'** – describe the way these yarns are arranged. The first fibre used for this purpose was cotton, but this was replaced by viscose, and now nylon (mainly), polyester and steel (as a fibre) are used.

△ Radial tyre – the basis is textiles

5.6 Leisure

We have seen textiles at work, but what about at play? The same properties of flexibility and toughness make them important here. Some examples:

1   **Tents**. When you are packing a fabric tent you might not think it easy to fold, but imagine what it would be like if it were made of any other material, except perhaps plastic, and that would tear easily.

2   **Sails**. For centuries, ships have relied on fabric sails, from the galleons of the sixteenth century to the sailing dinghies of today.

3   **Parachutes**. Not always leisure of course – sometimes a life saver. Parachutes need to be easily folded and then opened quickly, but must be tightly woven to hold the air under the canopy.

4   **Artificial sports surfaces**. These are like outdoor carpets that are unaffected by the weather, and are being used for all sorts of sports, from football to bowls. The first types had a pile of nylon, made like ribbons and coloured green to look like grass. Newer ones have a more felt-like top, and are used for artificial ski slopes. One advantage is that artificial surfaces cost a great deal less to maintain, and so are very popular with local authorities.

5.7 Artistic uses

Most textiles, and certainly clothing, have a decorative effect. To an artist, however, textiles may act as something they can use to express an idea or concept.

For a start, nearly all oil painters use a **canvas** – and that is a woven textile. But artists also use yarns and fabrics to create pictures and abstract designs. Perhaps the greatest of these are **tapestries**, originally woven to hang on walls in castles, monasteries and great houses.

△ The Bayeux Tapestry – an 11th century masterwork

A **collage** is a picture that may be built up from textile materials, pieces of fabric and yarn, and which gives a three-dimensional effect in many cases.

△ What no snow! – a textile ski-track

Macramé (knotted threadwork) uses textile yarn, and many artists use thread and small amounts of fibre to embroider pictures.

So the uses of textiles are very wide: from an artistic creation to an industrial filter cloth; from the hidden strength of a tyre to the folding of a parachute.

Summary

Textiles are not used only for clothes.

To begin with, there are many uses in the home – curtains, bedclothes and carpets, for example. In industry and outside the house the list grows even longer. Examples in industry include conveyor belts, tarpaulins, hoses, rope and filters. All uses rely on the flexibility combined with strength of textile yarns and fabrics.

Textiles are used for artificial sports surfaces, sails, tents, etc. They also form an essential base for tyres. To the artist, textiles may be used as a material for creating designs and pictures in a whole variety of ways.

Questions

1 Are these statements true or false?

   a Textiles are used only for clothing and in the home.

   b To do their job, car tyres depend on textile yarns.

   c Ropes are usually made from natural fibres.

   d Flocking and tufting are the same method of making carpets.

   e A tapestry is a picture painted on a textile canvas.

2 Complete the following:

   a _____ have taken the place of sheets and blankets as the top covering on beds.

   b The synthetic fibre most used for carpet backing is _____.

   c Ropes are made from plied yarns which are then _____ together.

   d _____ cloths are used to remove dust from the air in industry.

   e A 3D picture made of fabrics is called a _____.

3 Give three reasons why curtains might be lined.

4 a List three different cleaning items used in the home made from textile fibres.

   b Discuss whether these could be replaced by non-woven disposable items.

5 a List three types of carpet.

   b Describe the differences between them.

6 a What is an artificial sports surface?

   b What are the advantages and disadvantages of using such a surface?

7 Describe three ways in which textile materials are used in artistic creations.

8 You are going on holiday to the seaside by car, bus or train. List 10 items made entirely or partly from textiles which you might use or see (excluding clothes).

9 At a cement factory, the raw materials clay and limestone arrive as big lumps and have to be transported to grinders before being heated together in a furnace. The cement powder is then put into bags. The grinding process produces a lot of dust which has to be removed from the air. Cement is easily damaged if it gets wet before use and so it has to be carefully protected from rain when it is transported from the factory. Give three examples where items made completely or partly from textiles might be used in the factory, and for what purpose.

10 a Give five uses for rope or string.

   b Put these in order of strength required, starting with the weakest.

Design brief

You have been asked to decorate a
bedroom for a small child which he/she
also uses as a playroom. The room has a
bed, a fitted wardrobe, a chest of drawers
and a box for holding toys. Here are its
approximate sizes:

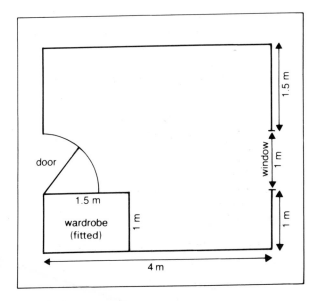

Redraw the room, showing your plan for it,
including the furniture.
 What materials or items would you use for
the wall covering, floor, bed linen and
curtains? You may choose textile items if
you wish, but you must discuss the reasons
for the choices you make and compare
these with alternatives.
▼   Give details of the construction of any
· textile items you use and suggest fibres
· they might be made from.
·   Draw and paint the patterns you would
▲ choose on each item.

6

What colour?

6.1 Elements of design

Life would be very dull without colour. Just imagine what it would be like, if we, like some animals, could see only black and white or shades of grey. But we mustn't think of colour in a negative way, we must think about it positively, because colour makes a real contribution to the way we see and appreciate clothes and textiles generally.

Colour is just one part of the way we enjoy and respond to what we see and feel when we look at clothing and textiles. The effect we see when we look at clothes includes such things as the line or shape, details of the fabric and the way the garment is made, and the texture or surface of the fabric.

▼ Let's look in more detail at some of these **elements** or parts that go to make up a **total design look**.

First, let's look at the lines of clothes. Any straight line tends to be hard and severe, and tends to suggest formal

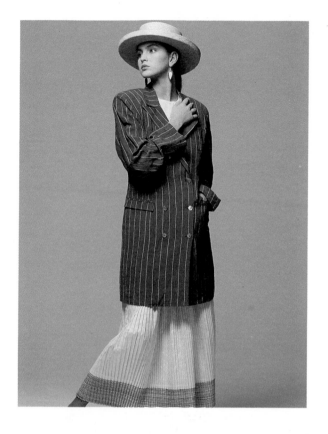

- clothes, such as the straight stripes or
- lines of a business shirt.
-     Curved lines are much more gentle,
- giving a flowing effect and sometimes a
- very rounded effect. Too much
- roundness, however, might give an effect
- we don't want – like looking a bit
- overweight.
-     Zig-zag lines can be very tiring to look
- at, but they give a rather startling effect –
- certainly the thing to use if you want to be
- noticed (like a flash of lightning,
- perhaps).
-     Even for straight lines, whether they
- are vertical or horizontal makes a
- difference. Vertical lines tend to create a
- slender, tall effect. Horizontal lines tend
- to exaggerate width (sometimes they may
- suggest lying down, and thus have a
- restful effect). So a tall, thin person might
- tend to wear horizontal lines, whereas a
- short, fat person would be better steering
- towards vertical ones.
-     A diagonal line gives the impression of

- movement. Notice how many athletes
- wear clothes with some sort of diagonal
- line or stripes across the body on them.
-     Another feature of the design is the
- form, or pattern. This can mean the
- overall shape of the clothes – big and
- solid, or fine and slender – or it can be
- the actual shapes of parts of, or patterns
- on, the clothes.

MINOAN · GOTHIC · RENAISSANCE · BAROQUE · BAROQUE · LOUIS XVI · 19th C. · 19th C.

- Every period of fashion has had its own
- distinctive overall shape – from
- Elizabethan and Victorian to the flappers
- of the 1920s, the mini skirts of the 1960s
- and the punks of the 1980s. Within this
- overall shape, however, there may be
- smaller details: the shape of the collar,
- the shape and the number of pockets, and
- the pattern on the fabric – is it plain or
- printed? what sort of print?
- An important part of the design is the
- background against which the shapes are
- seen. We could think of this in terms of a
- printed fabric. Imagine a floral print
- where a few small flowers are placed on
- a large, plain background. This can give
- a rather dainty, soft effect. Now imagine
- the same small flowers all closely packed
- together. We might say that such a print
- is 'busy'. It certainly doesn't have a quiet
- effect, and may be quite the reverse.
- Another part of the design is the
- texture. Is it smooth and flowing? Is it
- hard and knobbly? Of course, we
- appreciate texture by touch, but we can
- also see its effects. Smooth, shiny
- surfaces reflect light. Hard, knobbly ones
- do not, and tend to appear duller. Texture
- (or handle) is often associated with the
- fibres. Most people like the handle and
- texture of the natural fibres better than
- those of the man-made fibres, although
- some man-made fibres are so close to
- natural fibres that you can often be
- deceived. But think of the difference
- between smooth, shiny silk and the soft,
- uneven surface of wool. The texture
- affects the way we think about a textile –
- the soft, airy, floating of silk chiffon and
- the heavy, warm drape of a velvet
- curtain.

· Finally, we come to colour as part of
· the design effect. All the elements we
· have noted combine together for the
· overall effect with all the different colours
· – the reds, the greens, the yellows, and
· blues, and all the shades in between, not
· forgetting that white and black are
· colours, too. In the next section we look
· at colour, and how we see it, in more
▲ detail.

▽ Rainbow – sunlight passing through rain drops

6.2 **Seeing colour**

We can, of course, see colour only when there is a certain amount of light. At night there is usually some light about, if only the stars, and we can see outlines and shapes, but no colours. In an underground cave, however, if someone turns out the lights, we can see absolutely nothing.

The light from the sun contains all the colours; in a rainbow these are split up and we see the main colours of the **spectrum**:

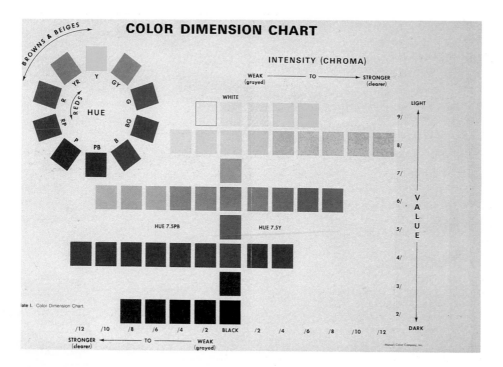

COLOR DIMENSION CHART

BROWNS & BEIGES

INTENSITY (CHROMA)

WEAK (grayed) — TO — STRONGER (clearer)

WHITE

HUE

REDS

LIGHT

9/

8/

7/

VALUE

6/

HUE 7.5PB   HUE 7.5Y   5/

4/

3/

2/

DARK

late I.   Color Dimension Chart.

/12   /10   /8   /6   /4   /2   BLACK   /2   /4   /6   /8   /10   /12

STRONGER (clearer) — TO — WEAK (grayed)

Munsell Color Company, Inc.

△ Hue circle on Munsell colour wheel

red, orange, yellow, green, blue and purple. So, to take an example, why are red peppers red and green peppers green? The reason is that when the light falls on them the skin of the red pepper absorbs all the light except the red, which is reflected back and so we see the pepper as red. The green pepper, however, absorbs all the red, orange and purple parts, but reflects back the green and most of the blue and yellow, and therefore appears green.

So that's how we see colour. Coloured fabrics absorb part of the light that falls on them and the combination of what they reflect back gives us the colour we see. The 'something' in the fabric which absorbs colour is the dye which we add to it.

One of the problems with light is that there is no such thing as constant light. Even sunlight varies, as you can see at dawn or at sunset, when the light is much redder. An ordinary electric light bulb is much more yellow than natural sunlight at midday, and, of course, some of the lights used for street lighting are very different colours again.

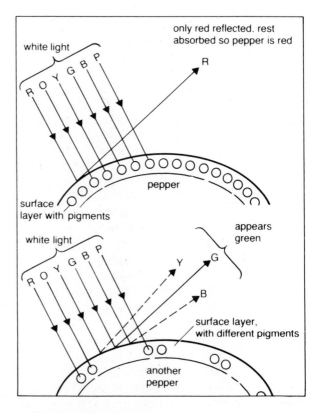

only red reflected. rest absorbed so pepper is red

white light

R O Y G B P

R

pepper

surface layer with pigments

appears green

white light

R O Y G B P

Y G

B

surface layer, with different pigments

another pepper

△ The pepper colour story

▼ For example, mercury lamps produce
· very little red light but a higher amount of
· blue and green, so if we looked at our
· peppers under a mercury lamp, the red
· ones would absorb all the colours and
· with no red to reflect, would appear
· black, whilst the green ones would
▲ appear noticeably more green.

This, of course, has a tremendous effect
when we are buying clothes, and if we
choose clothes that are the 'right' colour in
an artificially-lit shop they may look very
different in natural light. That's why you
have to be very careful.
Some advice to follow here is:

1 If you want a particular colour always
   look at it in daylight outside the shop if
   you can, and not just under the shop
   light.
2 If you want to match two colours, make
   sure they match in daylight as well as
   under shop light.

So you can see how we get colours and,
of course, from a textile fashion point of
view, black and white are colours, too.
White occurs where all the colours are
reflected, and black where they have all
been absorbed and nothing is reflected.
But there is more to colours than just red,
orange, yellow, green, blue and purple. We
all know there are many different tints and
shades, and colours may be very bright or
very dark.

▼ To represent this clearly, we need to
· think of colours in a more complicated
· way. Firstly, note that red, yellow and
· blue are called **primary** colours, and
· mixing them can give **secondary** colours
· – orange, green and purple.
· What we have called colour is usually
· referred to by scientists as **hue**. And we
· can arrange all the hues in a wheel-
· shaped diagram. Hues opposite each
· other on the wheel are known as
· complementary and if we mix them
· together we get a neutral grey. If we put
· two complementary hues side by side,
· however, they can produce a very

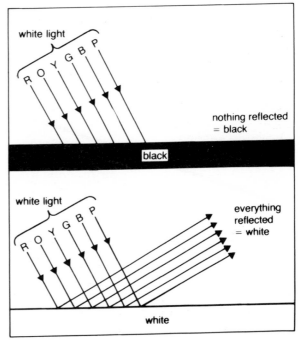

△ Black and white

· startling effect, a good example being the
· punk fashion of green hair with purple
· clothes. On the other hand, hues that are
· next to each other (analogous) do not
· produce a clash, and we say they go well
· together.
· But colours can also be light or dark,
· and this is referred to as their **value**. We
· can show this by putting a line down the
· centre of the wheel as an axle. On the
· axle itself, the extremes represent white
· and black. Adding white to a colour
· produces a lighter tint, while adding black
· gives a darker shade. Black objects ·
· absorb nearly all the energy which
· reaches them, which is why black always
· seems a hot colour in summer and white,
· which absorbs very little energy seems
· cool.
· Of course, we also get this effect with
· other hues: red, orange and yellow are
· considered warm, possibly because of
· their association with sun and fire,
· whereas the blues and greens are more
· restful. Red is a very strong colour,
· whereas green and blues seem rather to

- fade into the distance. We can think of
- this in terms of the uniforms of soldiers.
- The old British Army uniform in the
- seventeenth and eighteenth centuries
- was red, so that the soldiers could be
- easily seen and look strong; but this
- would have had a very bad effect on
- soldiers' chances of survival in modern
- warfare, so battle uniform has changed to
- blue-green and brown camouflage, in
- order to blend in with the surroundings
- and make the soldiers appear less
- obvious.
-    In terms of clothes, the use of
- contrasting colour values can have a
- great deal of effect. A black tie on a white
- shirt is a good example. This gives a
- strong effect, while a white dress with
- pale-coloured accessories has a very soft
- effect.
-    The third dimension of colour is its
- intensity. This describes how bright or
- dull the colour is. In scientific terms, this
- is termed **chroma**. On the wheel with the
- axis, we show this by the distance the
- colour is from the centre. Strong colours
- are on the outside; weaker colours are
- near the centre.
-    So, a particular colour has its own
- place on the colour wheel, and this place
- is worked out on the basis of different
- dimensions.
-    Colours close together on the wheel
- generally harmonize well, while colours
- at opposite extremes produce more
- startling effects and contrasts. The whole
- pattern of interaction of colours is very
- complicated. One reason for our reaction
- to colours is that we associate them with
- certain feelings. We talk about having the
- 'blues'; if we are angry, we see 'red'; we
- go 'green' with envy and 'purple' with
- rage. So, when we look at clothes, we
- respond to them in these terms, and if we
- want to express ourselves as being in a
- particular mood we can dress in a
- particular way, using particular colours.
-    Colours, therefore, not only give us an
- impression; they can express our
▲ feelings, too.

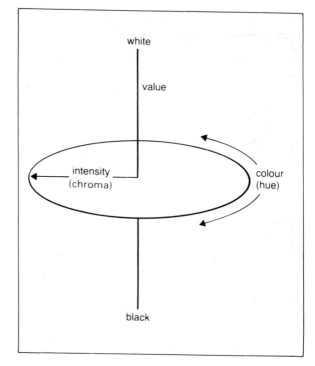

△ The Munsell colour wheel

6.3 Dyeing

As we have seen, a dye is a substance that
is added to a textile to give it colour. It does
this by the dye absorbing some of the white
light, what it reflects back being the colour
that we see. Of course, the dye isn't just
added to the textile in an unplanned way. To
start with, a dye has to be **fast**, that is, stay
on the textile to which it is added. If it didn't
do that it would come out in the first wash, if
not sooner. Different dyes are needed for
different colours, and sometimes dyes are
mixed to obtain exactly the right shade.

   There is another problem with the use of
dyes: different fibres require different
dyestuffs to produce the same colour. Many

people cannot understand why a dye that gives a good colour on cotton will not dye polyester – but why should it? Polyester is a different substance to cotton. What will stick to cotton will not necessarily stick to polyester, and vice versa. Dyers talk about different **classes** of dyestuffs – a class being a number of dyes that are suitable for a particular fibre. So, if you had a blend or mixture of fibres in a fabric, you might need to use two or more dyes to get a single colour – one for each fibre.

▼ The reaction between dyes and fibres is
· not chemical. If it were, dyestuffs might
· be faster against wearing and cleaning
· then they are. The bond between the fibre
· and the dyestuff is between the
· molecules, and is known as either
· hydrogen bond or Van der Waals forces.
· Only one class of dyestuff (reactive dyes)
· actually forms a chemical bond with the
▲ fibre it is used with (cotton).

Dyeing is nearly always carried out in a solution. The dye is dissolved in water, or suspended in it, and in a few cases dyeing can take place in the cold (some household dyes work this way). But in industry, to speed up the process, heat and sometimes pressure are usually used and other chemicals are added to the dyebath which help to open up the fibres to the dye.

In industry, the dyer carefully selects the dye and the amount to be used to give the exact shade required, and uses computers to match up one colour with another. But dyeing is not carried out on fabric alone; it can be done at different times in the textile process and, as a result, give different patterning effects. Let's look at how this works.

First of all, the *fibre* alone could be dyed. This is easily done. The loose fibres are put in a dyebath, and when a number of fibres have been dyed different colours they can be mixed together to give a heather or tweedy effect. Shetland sweaters are an example of where fibres are dyed and then mixed together before the yarn is spun.

fibre	main classes of dye stuff used
cotton	vat, reactive, direct
wool	acid
polyamide (nylon)	acid
polyester	disperse
acrylic	basic
viscose	vat

△ Fibre dyeing

Secondly, the *yarn* could be dyed. The problem here is that it is rather expensive, because the yarn cannot be thrown loose into the dyebath; it would get terribly tangled, and so it has to be wound on to a special package, unwound, and then re-wound after dyeing. But dyeing yarn is the way to get good, clean, stripe or check effects when different coloured yarns are woven or knitted into a fabric. Any bold check or stripe, for example in shirting, has probably been yarn dyed.

Thirdly, the *fabric* itself is dyed. Usually, the fabric length is joined end to end and it is put on a continuous sort of roller which takes it in and out of the dye bath. Fabric is normally dyed when a plain colour is required (this is called piece dyeing), but the method can be used to give a patterned effect. This is done by weaving or knitting two or more different fibres into the fabric and using only one sort of dyestuff so that only part of the fabric is dyed. This is known as cross dyeing, but it has to be done with care. The fibres used must be similar to each other in wearing, or the pattern may change as they wear differently. The most common type of cross dyeing uses nylon and polyester fibres in socks.

It isn't often done, but it is possible to dye the whole garment. The reason it is not often done is that for complicated garments with a lot of making up, the seams and the trimmings might be affected by the dyeing in a way that you don't want. However, garments with little making up are often dyed whole. Examples are stockings and tights, and quite a lot of knitwear. This method has big advantages for manufacturers, because they can wait until they know which colours are selling well before putting a lot of expensive material into the dye bath.

Imagine all the different ways of dyeing and the different ways of using dyed fibre and yarn to produce patterned fabric, and you can see how a tremendous variety builds up.

Before about 1870, there were very few dyes available. Only dyes from natural

△ Piece dyeing

▽ Cross-dyeing

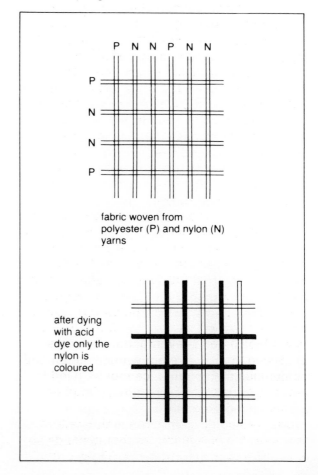

fabric woven from polyester (P) and nylon (N) yarns

after dying with acid dye only the nylon is coloured

sources, such as plants and a few animals, were available. Most of the shades were browns and yellows, and rather dull. The few bright colours were very expensive.

Since that time, however, thousands of man-made dyes have become available, mostly made from chemicals obtained from oil. (Probably the only natural dyestuff used in industry today is indigo blue, used for denim.) Just about every possible colour or shade of colour for any fibre is now available. If you add all these different colours to all the ways of producing pattern effects, you can see how a vast variety of fabrics can be built up. But even now we haven't finished, because there are still other ways of putting colour into textiles – in particular, printing.

6.4 Printing

It is possible to get complicated patterns by weaving and knitting, but another way of doing it is printing. For small designs and large, complicated patterns this can be cheaper than weaving or knitting with coloured yarns. Nearly all prints consist of colour laid on only one side of a fabric, so the reverse side is a plain colour, usually white. This does not matter as long as we take it into account when the garment is made up. Printing uses the same sort of dyestuffs as dyeing, but applies them to textiles in a different way.

The problem is to put the dye only where you want it, in the pattern you want, and not in any other place. One of the ways you may have used to do this yourself is **tie dyeing**. A piece of fabric or a T-shirt tied in a knot or bound up with strings is dipped into dyestuff. The knot or the strings restrict the flow of dye to parts of the garment, so that a blotchy or uneven pattern effect is produced. But tie dyeing, whilst it is fun and sometimes fashionable, cannot be used to create intricate or tiny patterns. Another method must be found.

One traditional way is to cut the pattern you want out of a block, so that it stands up in relief (you may have done this at school

with potatoes). Dye is then applied to the surface and the pattern printed on the fabric. You need one block for each colour and, to get a long length, a lot of labour, as you use the block up and down on the fabric many times. In industry, labour is too expensive to be used in this way, so the design is cut on a roller, and here we have the basis of one of the main industrial printing methods, **roller printing**. The rollers are usually made with a copper surface. They cost a lot to make, but last a long time. You need one roller for each colour, and big machines may have as many as 16 rollers, although two or three is more usual. For long runs (50,000 metres or more), rollers are very economical, but you do not get a very exact print, so the method is not good enough for the finest fabrics.

To get a very fine print you need to go on to the second big printing method, **screen printing**. A very fine screen, now usually made of nylon, is coated with a material that is dissolved away where you want the dye to go through, and this can be done very accurately by a photographic method.

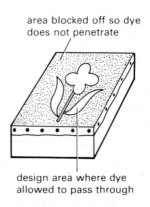

area blocked off so dye does not penetrate

design area where dye allowed to pass through

△ A simple print screen

Fine screens give very fine print. However, though not too expensive to produce, they can be easily damaged. The older method used flat screens, but in industry the screen is in the form of a cylinder so that it can be run over the fabric and give a continuous printing method. This is called **rotary screen printing**. You need one screen for each colour, but it can produce very detailed and intricate prints.

The newest method of printing seems at first glance to be rather a long way of doing it. The design is printed on paper, the paper is then placed next to a fabric, and the design is transferred by the action of heat. This is possible as the dyes that are used to print on the paper are specially chosen because they will come off the paper (sublime) in the form of a gas when heated, and so transfer to the fabric. Hence the name **transfer printing**. It seems a long way round, but it isn't really, because paper can be printed very fast (much faster than textile fabric) and with very intricate designs (think of some of the coloured pictures you have seen in papers and magazines). The method is used either with continuous rolls of paper and fabric, or with small motifs. You can do it yourselves at home or school by getting special transfer printing paint, painting it on to paper (spending all the time you like to get a beautiful design), and then transferring it on to fabric using heat. A domestic iron can be used for this purpose.

There is one drawback to transfer printing at present, which is that it works best on polyester and is not very good on most other fibres, especially wool and cotton. (Do not confuse transfer printing with the sort of transfers used as motifs on T-shirts. These are made of plastic, which softens on heating and sticks to the fabric.) Roller, rotary screen and transfer are the big three printing methods in industry, because they are relatively cheap and give the quality required.

Of course, there are many other printing methods which are used in art and craft work, or where the cost of labour is not too high. One of the most popular of these is

△ Screen printing speeded up

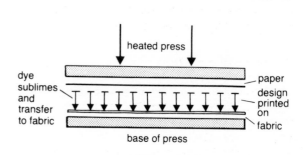

△ Transfer printing

batik. Batik solves the problem of letting the dye go only where you want it by coating the part of the fabric you don't want to print with wax. The wax is heated in a special container called a tjanting, and this is drawn over the fabric, coating the areas where the dye shouldn't go. The fabric is dyed, and then more wax is added and the process repeated to give another colour. Bold, striking designs can be produced, but it takes a long time and real batik is expensive to buy.

Printing adds a new dimension to getting colour on to fabrics. All the different colours available in dyestuffs are available to printers. Look around and you will see how they have taken advantage of them. Look, for example, at bed linen. A few years ago, most people had white sheets. Then, a few coloured sheets (plain) came on to the market. Now, most of us use duvets with printed colours, and the range of print designs is enormous. Just think how that has brightened our bedrooms.

6.5 **Other decoration**

Although dyeing and printing are the main ways of getting colour into a fabric, coloured designs can be put on fabric and garments by other methods.

One of these is **embroidery**, where threads of various colours are stitched into a pattern. Many domestic sewing machines can embroider patterns, and there are industrial embroidery machines. For many people, however, embroidery is something they enjoy doing by hand. Any part of a garment can be decorated, or even all over, but the hemline and the front are the parts most usually embroidered.

Designs can also be put on to a fabric or garment by **appliqué**. Here, small pieces of other fabrics are sewn by hand or machine on to the garment to build up the pattern. This could be an abstract design or a specific motif – for example, a flower.

Finally, any object, within reason, can be sewn on to a garment. Small pieces of metal, beads, rings, and of course badges

(that is, special designs woven on special machines using yarn and wire). These can denote membership of a club and, are used to a great extent on military and other uniforms.

The difficulty with all these types of special decoration is that they are relatively expensive. Even if not applied by hand, the machine work is very slow and this costs money; but you may think that it is still worthwhile to give that special, individual effect.

—————————— Summary ——————————

Colour puts life into textile items and is a vital part of the total design look.

The colour we see on textiles is the part of the spectrum that is not absorbed by the dye, and so is reflected back.

Dyes are chemicals added to textiles which can absorb some parts of the spectrum, and they have to be fast. Although the dye does not generally chemically combine with the fibre, it still has to form a bond by physical forces, and to do this a different class of dye is needed for each type of fibre.

Textiles can be dyed at all stages – fibre, yarn, fabric and garment, and the various methods have different pattern effects and different cost levels.

Dye is also used to print patterns on fabrics, the three main industrial methods being roller, rotary screen and transfer printing.

Questions

1 Are these statements true or false?
  a Coloured fabrics give off rays of light which we can see.
  b A fabric appears black because all the colours of the spectrum have been absorbed.
  c Textiles can be dyed only in fabric form.
  d Roller printing is best for intricate designs.
  e In transfer printing, the pattern is first printed on paper.

2 Complete the following.
  a Red, orange, yellow, green, blue and purple are colours of the
  _____.
  b When all the light is reflected back from a surface, the colour is _____.
  c _____ dyeing is used to get stripes and checks.
  d Wax is used to stop dye reaching parts of the fabric in _____ printing.
  e _____ is decoration using small pieces of fabric sewn on.

3 What effect can the following have on a garment?
  a vertical lines
  b horizontal lines
  c zig-zag lines

4 a List three methods of printing in industry.
  b Which of the following methods is likely to be used for printing?
    (i) a large amount of polyester fabric with a fine print
    (ii) a large amount of cotton fabric in a simple print
    (iii) a small amount of acrylic fabric in a fashion print

5 Colour is often the first thing that is noticed on an article. What are the following?
  a primary colours
  b secondary colours
  c complementary colours.
  What does 'value' mean in connection with colour?

6 Explain why, when you see a red fabric, you see it as red.

7 a List three stages at which colour can be put into textiles.
  b Describe the pattern effect which can result from each.

8 Coloured design can be put on to fabrics and garments by several methods. Describe how the following methods can be carried out.
  a embroidery
  b appliqué
  c tie dye
  d batik
  e transfer prints

9 a What is meant by 'classes' of dyestuffs?
  b Explain how this would affect the piece dyeing of a polyester/cotton fabric.

10 Explain how any colour is represented on a colour wheel.

Design brief

You have been asked to stage a fashion show with the following themes:

1 hot and vibrant
2 cool and restful

Sketch some items for a man and some for a woman to illustrate each theme.

(**Note:** You will need to show the lines of the clothes and any pattern, and to colour each item fully.)

7
How do we get textiles clean?

The old domestic chore of washing day has given way to the relatively easy use of automatic washing machines. We all know – or think we do – how we get dirty, but how do cleaning methods work? Why do we usually use a detergent from a packet instead of a bar of soap when we wash our clothes? What other methods are there? Will these change in the future?

7.1 How do we get dirty?

Ask anyone looking after children that question, and they will soon tell you. But are they thinking just about the mud and dust that children always manage to get on themselves when they fall over? If we think about it, dirt is a lot more complicated than that. There are many substances which get on to clothes and textile items which we want to remove; we call the dirtying process **soiling**, and how we get rid of it **cleaning**.

Soiling happens when we come into contact with dirt from two sources: both from ourselves, and from the outside.

Yes, we get *ourselves* dirty – from perspiration, from oil or grease from the skin, and from other excretions such as urine and faeces. And, of course, there is the soiling from outside – the dust that is everywhere, both on the ground and in the air (have you seen it in a beam of sunlight?); and then those accidents – falling in the mud, the make-up that went in the wrong place, the oil from the car, the spilt blackcurrant juice, etc.

Add all these up and what do you get? – a mixture of *different* soils – which suggests that one sort of cleaner will not get rid of all of them.

But which type do you think is the most common, the one that happens to all sorts of textile items that we wear and sleep in? Perspiration, yes, and oil and grease from the skin. And the biggest problem occurs

△ What on earth have you been doing to get that dirty?

where the oil and grease from the skin meet the dust from outside – collars, cuffs – around the edges generally; because the dust sticks to the grease. And don't forget that although some colours may not show the dirt so much, it's still there.

7.2 Washing

It would be easy if we could just brush off the soil from our clothes, but that's not enough; the oil and grease stop that from happening, so we need to remove the oil and grease – we need to dissolve it – and we need to do it cheaply because we do it a lot.

What's the cheapest substance we know of that dissolves things? – water.

But does water work to clean clothes? – the answer is no, not by itself. To illustrate this, put some oil on your hands and then dip them in water; the oil stays on your hands and the water forms drops on top of it. Water needs something additional to help remove oil and grease – and that something is a **detergent**.

The best known detergent is, of course, soap, which is made from natural products; but most detergents used for washing textiles are produced from chemicals obtained from oil. These substances are usually called synthetic detergents, to distinguish them from soap. Well-known brands – on every supermarket shelf – are Persil, Surf, Bold etc., and the big supermarkets like Sainsbury's, Tesco and Safeway have their own brands.

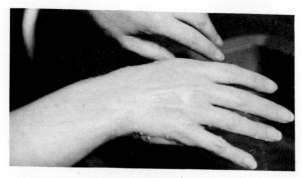

△ Water meets grease – stalemate

▼ Soap is made from fats and oils. It used to be made from animal fats, but nowadays mostly vegetable or plant oils are used – for example, oil from palm and coconut trees and from cotton seeds. The oil is treated with caustic soda to produce soap which is separated and purified. When you buy soap, it has usually been compressed (squeezed) to remove water and then formed into bars. Some colouring and perfume may be added, and occasionally deodorant or mild disinfectant, and it often has a fancy package. A small amount of soap is made as flakes and sold for hand washing of clothes (e.g. Lux).

Synthetic detergents are built up (synthesized) from simple chemicals obtained from oil, and are usually produced as a powder. They are different chemical compounds from soap, but certain parts of the soap molecule are similar to synthetic detergent molecules, and it is those parts which enable both to
▲ act as detergents.

Detergents

▼ We have seen how water on its own forms drops on oil or grease, so the first job the detergent must do is to allow the water to soak into the fabric. It does this by reducing the tension around the surface of the water droplet.

After this, the special way a molecule of detergent is made comes into play. The two ends of a molecule of detergent have different properties; one end is attracted to water and the other to oil or grease, so the detergent acts as a sort of bridge between the dirt and the water to enable the dirt to be lifted off the surface of the material.

To do all this the detergent is helped by energy, which is available in two ways – from the water (the higher the temperature the more energy is available), and from agitation (your hands or the paddle action of a washing
▲ machine).

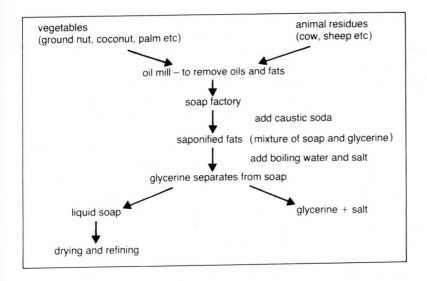

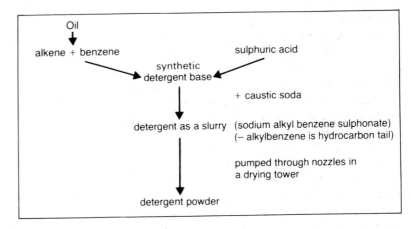

▽ The detergent molecule at work

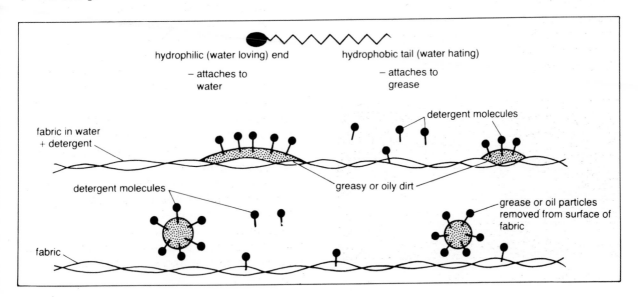

The basic principles of washing are water plus detergent, a container, heat and agitation.

All we need now are: a means of rinsing, to get the detergent and the attached dirt away; a way of drying, to get rid of the water; and a way of straightening out any creases – ironing or pressing.

But these come later. Before we look at any of that, let's go back to detergents. Do they work? Well, yes, in part. A detergent used correctly will remove most, if not all, of the body oil or grease and with it much of the dust, but as we saw these are not the only types of soiling which might be on the textile. A detergent alone may not be sufficient to remove all the different kinds of dirt.

That is why, when you buy a packet of what we call 'detergent', it does not contain just a simple cleaning agent (i.e. the detergent); it also contains a number of other substances designed to increase the range of soils that can be removed, and to add to the appearance of textiles after washing.

▼ This means that a packet of detergent is a **formulated** product.
   First, there is the detergent itself (called the **surfactant** by the manufacturer), but this may be as little as 15 per cent of the total. It is usually a synthetic detergent, because these have an important advantage over soap: they are not affected by the **hardness** of the water.

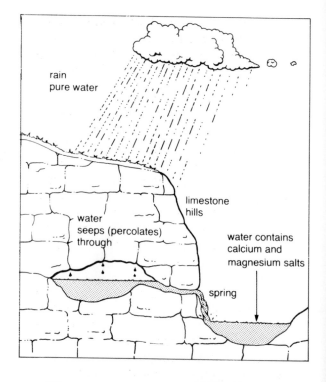

rain
pure water

limestone
hills

water
seeps (percolates)
through

water contains
calcium and
magnesium salts

spring

When rain falls on certain rocks, such as chalk and limestone, it dissolves small amounts of calcium and magnesium salts. After the rain is collected in a reservoir, and even after it has been through the waterworks and purified, these salts remain; so if you live in an area where the water in the tap comes from rain collected in chalk or limestone, the water will contain these salts – and it will be 'hard'. You can see the results of hard water in the 'fur' that forms in kettles and, in particularly bad cases, the deposits that block up water pipes and steam irons.

When soap is used with hard water it reacts with these salts and forms a precipitate (or solid scum), which leaves deposits on the clothes and uses up soap so that it is not available for cleaning. Synthetic detergents, however, do not react with hard water in this way. Even so, a **water softener** (that is, a chemical which will remove water hardness) is usually added to detergent packs; this can be as much as 30 per cent of the total, and also helps to remove dirt.

I'm **formulated!**
I've detergent & water softner & **bleach** & optical **brightness**...

The detergent used also depends on what sort of washing machine you have. Automatic machines can be blocked by too much lather, so a special **low-lather** detergent is needed. So use only detergents marked 'low lather' or 'for automatic machines' if you have an automatic washer.

For some stains which are not removed by the detergent, a **bleaching** agent is added. Bleaching agents break down certain dyes or colours so that they do not show. Of course, this must be a mild bleaching agent, or it might damage the textiles. This may amount to as much as 20 per cent of the product.

Another substance is added which takes no part in the cleaning process at all. This may account for up to a quarter of the pack and is a substance which is there simply to absorb water and keep the whole detergent pack dry, so that when you pour the powder into the washing machine it flows freely.

There are also some substances added in smaller amounts to help keep the dirt away from the textile once it has been removed, to help the lather and to hold the granules of detergent together, thus stopping them going into too fine a powder.

But there is one other important agent which is added only in small quantities, and that is an **optical brightening agent** (sometimes called a **fluorescer**). Such substances work by absorbing ultra-violet light from daylight and emitting it again as white light, and it is these which give the whiter than white appearance about which the detergent advertisers talk so much. They do not make the clothes any cleaner, they just make them look whiter and brighter.

But there are still some soils which may not be totally removed. We have seen how the detergent removes most, if not all, of the oil- or grease-based soil, the water itself will remove any soil which will dissolve in it, and the bleaching agent may remove some of the dyes or coloured soils, but that leaves

△ They've forgotten to get low lather detergent again!

soils such as blood or urine which contain chemicals called **proteins**. These are resistant to all these other agents, and to remove them many detergents now contain substances called **enzymes**, which attack protein soils, break them ▲ down, and help to remove them.

The detergent pack may contain a **softening** agent (e.g. Bold 3). This is a special type of detergent which remains on the fabric after it has been dried and lubricates the fibres so that the handle is softer. If they are not in the detergent pack, softeners are often added to the final rinse. This type are usually sold as **fabric conditioners** (e.g. Comfort, Lenor, etc.).

So a detergent pack is very complicated, and it is likely to get more complicated as more substances are added to widen the range of soils that can be removed, especially as detergents are used at lower and lower temperatures.

Detergents are developing all the time. Sometimes the changes do not improve the cleaning, but just make the detergent easier to use. For example, liquid detergents for washing clothes are now being sold (Wisk, Ariel Liquid etc.) instead of the traditional powder. These should not be confused with the liquid detergents sold for washing dishes (Fairy Liquid, Palmolive Liquid, Sunlight etc.), which do not give such good results with clothes because they are not specially formulated for that purpose.

Even after washing in detergent, all the dirt may not be removed and it may be necessary to use special cleaning agents for stubborn spots and stains. Each particular stain may require different treatment. The table gives a list of some of the more common and how to remove them, but be careful; always check to make sure you do not damage the material or any dye it may contain.

adhesives	white spirit*	**grass**	methylated spirit
ballpoint ink	methylated spirit	**lipstick**	white spirit*
blood	hydrogen peroxide or soak in enzyme based detergent	**mildew**	hydrogen peroxide
butter/margarine	white spirit*	**milk**/ice cream nail polish	detergent + white spirit* acetone, amyl acetate (sold as nail polish remover)
chewing gum	freeze to remove as much as possible (it becomes brittle) then white spirit*	oil	white spirit*
		paint–emulsion	cold water + detergent
coffee/tea	hydrogen peroxide	**paint**–other	white spirit*
fruit juice	hydrogen peroxide	**tar**	white spirit*

notes:

wash as normal after removing stain

*white spirit is a mixture of organic solvents – special stain removers like Dabitoff can be used instead

hydrogen peroxide is a mild bleach, sodium perborate can be used instead

methylated spirits is (ethyl) alchohol with dye and other chemicals added which makes it **poisonous** to drink

do not use nail polish remover on acetate fabric (it dissolves!)

remember – *with any stain remover test its effect on a 'corner' of the fabric first.*

Washing machines

In the last section we saw the basis of washing – water plus detergent, a container, heat and agitation. The simplest form of washing to combine these features is by hand: water – from the tap; container – bowl or basin; heat – hot water, either from the hot tap heated by the domestic heating system, or from a kettle (the maximum temperature the hand can bear is 50°C, and some may find that a little too hot); agitation – by hand action.

A washing machine is designed to make washing a whole lot easier, but the *principle* is just the same. The only difference is that, once set by you, the machine takes over and does all the work, including the rinsing and, in some cases, all the drying.

Simple washing machines were available before World War II, but from 1950 onwards new designs constantly appeared as more and more people began to own machines.

Let's look in more detail at the jobs which have to be done after the cleaning part of washing, which can sometimes be done by machines.

Rinsing – after washing, the dirt is in the water with the detergent, and this has to be removed and the textiles soaked in clean water to remove all traces of dirt and detergent. This may have to be done several times, sometimes using hot water, to dissolve all the left-over detergent, and we may add conditioner at this stage. This, as we saw earlier, is the special type of detergent which is intended to stay on the fabric (which is one reason why it goes in the last rinse), to make it feel softer.

Drying – after the items have been rinsed, they are still wet. To remove the water requires energy – but where does it comes from? With wringing – twisting the item between the hands – you provide the energy (but be careful; wringing may damage delicate fabrics). If items are hung outdoors on a line, to begin with the weight of the water itself causes it to run out, then the wind and the sun provide the energy to remove the rest. Indoors, the heat of the room is used, perhaps by hanging in front of the fire or radiator (although great care is needed – don't use an open fire). An old system, rarely seen today, was the wringer or mangle, where the textile was squeezed between two rollers.

Most people today use a **spin dryer**. The textiles are put inside a drum which rotates at high speed. The force, as the textiles are flung to the outside of the drum, removes the water (although not always completely). In a **tumble dryer**, the textiles are again put inside a drum, but when it rotates, hot air from a heater passes over the textiles and dries off the water (tumble dryers use a lot of electricity, however, and are expensive to run).

There are three main types of washing machine in use today:

1   Twintubs. These have a separate washer and spin dryer. When washing you usually have to reset the machine for rinsing when the wash cycle has finished, and the rinsed clothes then have to be transferred to the spin dryer.

▽ A typical twin-tub

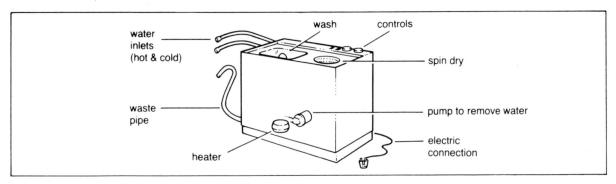

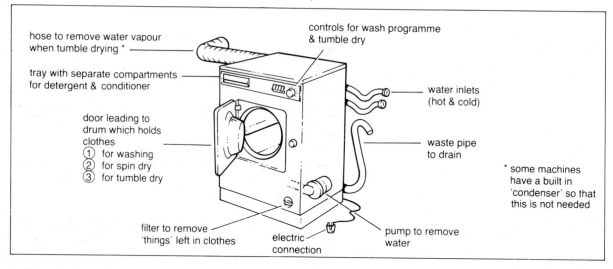

hose to remove water vapour
when tumble drying *

tray with separate compartments
for detergent & conditioner

door leading to
drum which holds
clothes
① for washing
② for spin dry
③ for tumble dry

controls for wash programme
& tumble dry

water inlets
(hot & cold)

waste pipe
to drain

* some machines
have a built in
'condenser' so that
this is not needed

filter to remove
'things' left in clothes

electric
connection

pump to remove
water

△ The whole works – automatic wash/dryer

2 Automatic washing machines. You load the machine with clothes, add detergents and conditioner (if used) in special compartments, set the program and the machine does the rest, including rinsing and spinning.

3 Automatic washer/dryer. This does all an automatic washer does, but includes a built-in tumble dryer. You usually have to reset the machine after spinning to use the tumble dryer.

Wash codes

All automatic washing machines offer you a choice of programs, that is a number of different washing conditions. But why? Detergents need heat and agitation to work, so why not use one set of washing conditions which suit the detergent?

The answer is that the washing conditions also have to suit the textile item that is being washed, and some textiles have to be treated very carefully.

But how do you, the consumer, know what conditions to use? You must rely on the manufacturer of the item to tell you, preferably by putting a label on the item giving the correct washing instructions.

The scheme which has been operated in the UK since the mid 1960s was devised by a committee made up of leading fibre, textile, clothing, washing machine and detergent manufacturers. It was first called

the HLCC (Home Laundering Consultative Committee) scheme, but is now known as the **ICLC (International Care Labelling Code)** since it became used in many other parts of the world in the 1970s. It has recently been revised (British Standard 2747: 1986), and the new symbols will be seen increasingly, but the old code is likely to be with us for some time.

The old and new codes are given in the table. The code is often printed on the sides of detergent packets, and the programs and how to use them are listed in the instruction books for most washing machines.

The main basis of the old code are nine washing programs which are indicated by a diagram of a wash tub containing one of the numbers 1 to 9. In addition, there is a handwash only program. Each code number corresponds to a set of instructions about:

1 The washing temperature
2 How much agitation the fabric can take
3 Rinse temperature
4 Drying

The new code has fewer symbols, and these are not numbered. Instead, the only number in the wash tub is the water temperature. The amount of agitation is shown by lines under the wash tub – no lines meaning normal, one line reduced and two lines highly reduced.

Many manufacturers use instruction labels sewn into textile items either at the neck, on the inside of a trouser pocket or in a side seam. On small items, the code may be printed on the ticket attached to the item when it is sold, or perhaps on the bag holding it. Sometimes, the wash tub symbol only is displayed.

For some fibres, more than one code is possible (for example, for cotton), because of the possibility of dyes not being fast at various temperatures. If in doubt, use the least severe conditions (the highest number on the old code).

The idea of the code was that the person doing the washing could sort their textile items into a series of piles based on the washing conditions required. They would then wash each pile separately, either by putting it into an automatic washing machine and setting the right program according to the instructions, or, with a non-automatic machine, by using the controls to obtain the correct conditions. (Except, of course, for the hand-washing pile.)

Examples of application

	MACHINE	HAND WASH
1 95	Very hot to boil maximum wash	Hand-hot or boil
	Spin or wring	

White cotton and linen articles without special finishes

	MACHINE	HAND WASH
2 60	Hot maximum wash	Hand-hot
	Spin or wring	

Cotton, linen or rayon articles without special finishes where colours are fast at 60°C

	MACHINE	HAND WASH
3 60	Hot medium wash	Hand-hot
	Cold rinse Short spin or drip-dry	

White nylon; white polyester/cotton mixtures

	MACHINE	HAND WASH
4 50	Hand-hot medium wash	Hand-hot
	Cold rinse Short spin or drip-dry	

Coloured nylon; polyester; cotton and rayon articles with special finishes; acrylic cotton mixtures; coloured polyester/cotton mixtures

	MACHINE	HAND WASH
5 40	Warm medium wash	Warm
	Spin or wring	

Cotton, linen or rayon articles where colours are fast at 40°C, but not at 60°C

	MACHINE	HAND WASH
6 40	Warm minimum wash	Warm
	Cold rinse Short spin Do not wring	

Acrylics; acetate and triacetate, including mixtures with wool; polyester/wool blends

	MACHINE	HAND WASH
7 40	Warm minimum wash	Warm Do not rub
	Spin Do not hand wring	

Wool, including blankets and wool mixtures with cotton or rayon; silk

	MACHINE	HAND WASH
8 30	Cool minimum wash	Cool
	Cold rinse Short spin Do not wring	

Silk and printed acetate fabrics with colours not fast at 40°C

	MACHINE	HAND WASH
9 95	Very hot to boil maximum wash	Hand-hot or boil
	Drip-dry	

Cotton articles with special finishes capable of being boiled but requiring drip drying

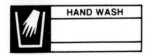

	HAND WASH

Articles which must not be machine washed. Details will vary because garment manufacturers are free to put their own written instructions on this label

Do not wash

△ ICLC scheme

Table 1. Washing symbols

Symbol	Required phrase	Description of process
95	'Wash in cotton cycle' or 'Wash in cotton programme' or 'Wash as cotton'	Maximum temperature of wash : 95 °C Mechanical action normal Rinsing normal Spinning normal*
60	'Wash in cotton cycle' or 'Wash in cotton programme' or 'Wash as cotton'	Maximum temperature of wash: 60 °C Mechanical action normal Rinsing normal Spinning normal*
50	'Wash in synthetics cycle' or 'Wash in synthetics programme' or 'Wash as synthetics'	Maximum temperature of wash: 50 °C Mechanical action reduced Rinsing with gradual cooling before spinning Spinning reduced*
40	'Wash in cotton cycle' or 'Wash in cotton programme' or 'Wash as cotton'	Maximum temperature of wash: 40 °C Mechanical action normal Rinsing normal Spinning normal*
40	'Wash in synthetics cycle' or 'Wash in synthetics programme' or 'Wash as synthetics'	Maximum temperature of wash: 40 °C Mechanical action reduced Rinsing with gradual cooling before spinning Spinning reduced*
40	'Wash in wool cycle' or 'Wash in wool programme' or 'Wash as wool'	Maximum temperature of wash: 40 °C Mechanical action much reduced Rinsing: normal Spinning normal* Do not wring by hand
(hand)	Hand wash	Hand wash Do not machine wash Maximum temperature of wash: 40 °C Wash time: short Wash, rinse and gently squeeze by hand Do not wring
(crossed out)		Do not wash

*If the article is to be drip dried, remove from machine before final spin.

Although the codes give a guide for drying (e.g. spinning) tumble drying is not included. This is because most people did not have tumble dryers in the 1960s, when the old code was introduced. There are, however, special symbols for tumble drying, and some manufacturers use them; these are shown in the table.

There is another symbol you may see on textiles, and this is about bleaching; occasionally, the words 'do not bleach' are written on the label.

Bleaches are chemicals which can destroy colour and so make an item appear whiter. This colour may be a soil that you do not want to be there, or it may be a colour which is part of the textile. So bleaches have to be used with great care, and generally only on normally white items which have got particularly dirty. Even then, there are still precautions to be taken. Some fibres (especially wool and silk) can be badly damaged by strong bleaches.

For these reasons, bleaching agents or chemicals are rarely used in the UK as cleaning agents for textiles (though they are, of course, widely used in both the home and industry for destroying bacteria). A mild (weak) bleaching agent is, however, included in detergent formulation. If you do decide to use a bleach to get textiles clean, always take care.

1 Read the instructions carefully so that you use the right strength.
2 Wear rubber gloves.
3 Avoid splashes, especially on skin and in the eyes.

If in any doubt, *do not* use bleach.

The table shows the symbols you may see about bleaching.

Drying (after washing) symbols		
Symbol	Optional phrase	Description of process
▢	Tumble dry	Articles which are suitable for tumble drying
⊠	Do not tumble dry	Articles which may not be tumble dried

Chlorine-based bleaching symbols		
Symbol	Optional phrase	Description of process
△ Cl	May be chlorine bleached	Bleaching (chlorine-based)
⧄	Do not chlorine bleach	Do not use chlorine-based bleach

7.3 Dry cleaning

We saw in section 7.2 that water by itself will not dissolve oil and grease – but there are liquids that will. If the oil or grease goes, anything attached to it, such as dust, goes too. The liquids used for this purpose are specially chosen organic **solvents** (that is, liquids which will dissolve something).

▼ The solvents used are chosen because
· they are not poisonous, are not
· flammable and, of course, have a good
· cleaning action. Over the years several
· solvents have been used, more recently
· perchloroethylene and trichloroethylene.
· At present a new solvent,
· trichlorotrifluoroethane (known as Solvent
· 113), is being increasingly used. Some
· dry cleaner shops advertise that they use
· this solvent under the trade name
▲ Arklone.

The textile item is 'washed' in the organic solvent in a machine rather like a domestic washing machine, but it is a lot more complicated than that. There are two reasons for this. Firstly, an organic solvent cannot be poured down the drain like water, because it could cause a serious pollution problem. So the machine has to have a special recovery system, which is expensive. Secondly, the solvent costs a lot more than water, which is another reason for not putting it down the drain.

The special equipment and the care needed in using the solvent make dry cleaning impractical in the average home, so it has to be done in a factory or specially equipped dry cleaning shop or coin-op launderette. This means that it is expensive compared with washing. If you do have an item dry-cleaned, and especially if you do it yourself at a coin-op, always air the item before wearing or using it – just to make sure all the solvent is removed.

Why dry clean? Well, it has three big advantages.

1 Wool items which would shrink if washed can generally be dry cleaned without problems.
2 Dry cleaning is less likely to cause dyes to run, so it can be used for items which have poor dye fastness when washed.
3 It is very good at removing oil and grease, so that items heavily soiled with these often achieve a better result with

dry cleaning than with washing. On the other hand, dry cleaning will not remove every type of soil, and the range of soils which can be removed by the latest types of detergent is wider.

As for washing, there are symbols to go on labels to show whether an item can be dry cleaned or not, and these are given in the table.

Dry cleaning symbols	
Symbol	Optional phrase and description
Ⓐ	**Dry clean** Can use all solvents normally used for dry cleaning
Ⓟ	**Dry clean** Use perchloroethylene solvent 113. solvent 11 and hydrocarbons (white spirit) using the normal dry cleaning procedures
Ⓟ̲	**Dry clean** As above but with restrictions on cleaning procedures
Ⓕ	**Dry clean** Use solvent 113 and hydrocarbons only using the normal dry cleaning procedures
Ⓕ̲	**Dry clean** As above but with restrictions on cleaning procedures
⊗	**Do not dry clean**

7.4 Ironing and pressing

When textiles have been washed (or for that matter, dry cleaned), they end up creased to some degree. How much creasing occurs depends on a number of things: the fibre or fibres the item is made from; the way the fabric is made up; the way the garment or other item is put together; and the washing or cleaning conditions.

Sometimes there is so little creasing that the item could be called 'no iron' or perhaps 'minimum iron' – both slogans used by manufacturers and retailers. Sometimes, however, the item is so badly creased that it looks like a screwed-up ball and obviously needs heavy and careful ironing. But most items need at least a 'touch' with an iron. Why? – because, of course, we want to return the item as far as possible to look as it did when it was new.

There are sometimes occasions when we want the item to stay creased! That is, when it contains a crease or pleat which is part of the style of the garment – for example, in a pair of trousers. Then we press to keep the crease or pleat in (you can see here an example of confusion – we use the word crease to describe both something we want and something we don't want).

In the home, ironing is carried out in the same way as it is done when making up (see Chapter 4). The iron settings are sometimes shown on garment labels, but if not, the fibre content label is used as a guide to the right setting. If the fabric is a blend, use the lowest setting, i.e. the one which is needed for the most sensitive fibre present.

In industrial laundries and dry cleaners, irons are used for small items but take too long for larger garments, and so presses are used. A Hoffman steam press is the sort normally used (see Chapter 4). A version of the Hoffman press has been produced for domestic use, but few houses have room for one and they are not very popular.

Summary

We all get dirty, and the dirt comes partly from ourselves and partly from outside. This dirt consists of a whole lot of different things, but will include grease.

Water cannot remove grease on its own, so we need to use a detergent with it. This may be soap or a synthetic detergent.

The detergent powders used for washing contain a mixture of substances to make removal of dirt easier and to improve the appearance of textiles after washing. This is why these work better than ordinary soap, especially when used in hard water (water containing calcium and magnesium salts).

In the home, most washing is done in a washing machine which controls the water temperature, automatically rinses and partly dries the clothes.

It is necessary to use different washing conditions for different items, not only because of the soil on them but because of the different fibres, fabrics and dyes used.

To help with this, we have the International Care Labelling Code, with its wash tub symbols. Labels in textile items may contain this code and advice on tumble drying, bleaching, dry cleaning and ironing.

Dry cleaning is another method of cleaning. It uses organic solvents to dissolve the grease and can be very efficient, but not for all types of soil. Dry cleaning cannot be done in the home.

When textiles have been cleaned, they will probably need ironing or pressing. The usual method in the home is a domestic iron, but care must be taken or certain fabrics may be damaged.

Questions

1 Are these statements true or false?

  a Soap is a detergent.
  b Water dissolves greasy soil and removes the dust which has stuck to it.
  c Dry cleaning uses organic solvents to dissolve grease.
▼ d An automatic washing machine uses any type of detergent.
· e Enzymes are the only detergents which will remove all stains.
▲

2 Complete the following:

  a There are _____ different wash codes in the old international care labelling scheme.
  b There are _____ different heat settings on the average domestic iron.
  c A _____ agent can destroy colour as well as dirt on a garment.
  d A _____ dryer uses heat to dry clothes.
▼ e _____ are added to detergent packs to give a whiter than white appearance after washing.
▲

3 a There are three main ways in which clothes may be cleaned:

    a at home
    b sending to a laundry or dry cleaners
    c using a launderette

  Give two advantages and two disadvantages of each method.

4 What method of coping with the laundry would you recommend for each of the following situations?

  a an elderly person living alone
  b a student living in a hostel with no drying facilities
  c a family with two young children living in a remote place

Give reasons for each recommendation.

5 Most households today have either an automatic washing machine or a twin tub.

  a Explain the main differences between the two types.
  b List the advantages and disadvantages of each machine.

6 What do the following mean?

  a HLCC
  b ICLC

Give two advantages of a care labelling scheme.

7 A code of care is based on the following four symbols. Explain each one.

8 a What are:
▼
·   (i) fabric softeners?
    (ii) water softeners?

· b When are they used in washing in
▲   the home?

9 a Name three substances found in the home (other than detergents) which could be used to remove stains.

  b For each substance, state one stain which it could help remove and name a fabric on which it could be safely used.

10 You decided to buy an iron for someone setting up home. Explain the factors which would affect your final choice.

11 a List three ingredients of detergent
▼   packs.

· b What are their main uses in
▲   washing?

12 a List four operations of an automatic washing machine.
  b Put them in order in the wash cycle.

_____ Design brief _____

List ten types of fabrics, and items made from them, which you think are the most important textiles (clothes and household) used today. You must include the fibres.

Group them together where you think that they could normally be cleaned together.

Find a suitable washing program under the new code which would suit each of your new groups. (If you are unsure, use the old code as a guide.)

Add ironing and tumble drying instructions to your list.

▼ When you have completed the code for
· your list, carry out a survey amongst other
· pupils to see if they understand what the
· symbols mean. Based on this, write a
▲ criticism of the new code.

8

What do we want from textiles?

The first requirement for many people may be that the textiles they use should look good, but that is not the whole story. They must also stand up to the way we use and clean them – and this does not happen by accident. For something to be 'washable', for example, certain properties must be built in from the beginning. What are these properties and how do we measure them?

8.1 Performance

A good performance means that the textiles do the things we want them to do – in other words, that they stand up to the wear or use and cleaning that we give them. If you think about the properties you expect you might come up with a list something like this (the words in brackets are a more scientific way of expressing these properties):

Lasts a long time (**durable**)
Does not shrink, or extend (**dimensional stability**)
Keeps its shape – does not crease, go baggy, lose pleats (**shape retention**)
Dries quickly (**hydrophobic**)
Colours do not run (**dye fast**)
Keeps you warm, or cool (**insulation**)
Doesn't burn (**flame retardant**)

You may have used phrases like '**minimum iron**' or '**easy-care**'. These are another way of saying 'keeps its shape', because if it does this in wear and washing, the item needs little or no ironing.

You may have said '**washable**', but that's another way of saying that you do not want the item to change size (shrink or extend) or lose colour when it's washed. The words '**machine washable**' simply mean that you can use a machine and get the same result.

There are three points to note about performance properties:

1 The properties you look for vary with the item you buy – for example, you may not worry too much about durability for a special occasion garment, but you are more likely to for a pair of trousers. Resistance to fire may be more important on a curtain than on a T-shirt.

2 Sometimes you may not be able to get everything you want, and you may have to decide to put up with something you don't like. For example, you may want a special fashion colour, but you may have to accept that that colour runs and that you will have to hand wash it separately. On the other hand, somebody else may insist on machine washability and so go for the less fashionable colour.

3 All performance properties result from the way the textile item is made, and they can all be understood in scientific or technical terms – unlike the 'look' of the item, which may *result* from the way it is made but can only be *understood* in aesthetic terms.

▼ How a textile item performs depends on the various forces holding it together – so what are those forces?
First, we have the molecules of the fibre; these consist of atoms held together by chemical forces. Then there are the fibres themselves; these are molecules held together by inter-molecular forces (hydrogen bonds or Van der Waals forces).
The yarns are made up of fibres, which are held together by physical forces – friction, as a result of the way the yarn is made (lining up the fibres and putting in twist).

- Fabric is made up of yarns held
- together by forces between the yarns –
- the friction between the yarns as they
- interlace in a woven fabric, and the
- strength of the yarns as they form loops
- in a knitted fabric.
- Finally, the garment or textile item is
- held together by the seams which join the
- pieces of fabric together, the strength
- coming from the fabric, the sewing thread
- and the way the stitch is formed.
- So a textile item is held together by
- many different forces. Some of these may
- be strong, and some may be weak, and
- the whole thing is only as strong as its
- weakest link. For example, a very strong
- fabric made from a strong fibre can make
- a useless garment if the seams break the
- first time we wear it because of weak
- sewing thread.
- When we wear or use a textile item,
- various things can happen to it which can
- test the forces holding it together. For
- example, perspiration produces
- chemicals which can break down the
- molecules of certain fibres – and this
- leads to rotting. When we rub a fabric, if
- the yarn is not well made and the fibres
- can pull loose, the fabric becomes fluffy,
- and in the end the fibres may all work
▲ loose to leave a hole.

8.2 **Testing**

If a property such as durability is important
to us, we must have some way of testing it,
or at least the manufacturer should be able
to test it before it goes on sale.

The obvious way to test a textile item is
for someone to use it! But think about it –
people use things differently, so a lot of
people would have to use something before
we could be certain of the results, and
some things, such as durability, might take
a long time to test. So wearer trials, as they
are called, are not often used.

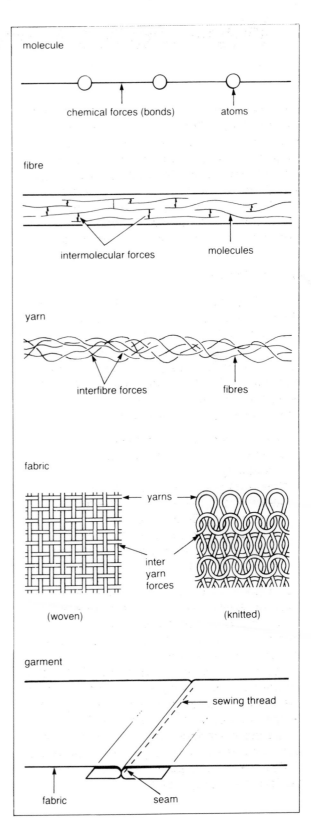

△ Universal tester

What, then, can we do instead? We can invent tests to carry out in a laboratory which copy as far as possible what actually happens in use. This is not always easy, but such tests do give results which can be used to decide whether or not a textile will be satisfactory in use. For example, will it shrink on washing, will the colour run, and how much ironing will it need?

▼ The whole laboratory testing
· requirements can be summarized as
· follows:

· **1** The test must copy, as far as possible,
· what happens in real life.
· **2** The test must give reproducible
· results – meaning that different people
· testing the same fabric get the same
· results.
· **3** There must be a definite
· measurement, i.e. a number or
· numerical value, that comes from the
· test.
· **4** Having got a result, we must have an
· idea of what we will accept, and this
· will, of course, vary, depending on the
· item we are considering. For example,
· we will look for a high value for
· durability on a school blazer, but
▲ accept a lower value on a fashion top.

8.3 Durability

If a hole or a break appears in the fabric or the seam of a textile item this means trouble, and we have either to throw it away or to mend it. Mending may mean re-sewing a seam, sewing on a patch, or darning, which is way of working yarn backwards and forwards over a hole. So-called invisible mending takes yarn or fabric from a part of a garment that does not show and uses it to mend a hole or a tear where it does show. It requires a great deal of skill, takes a long time and is expensive.

But how do the holes or tears get there in the first place? That is very complicated, because a lot of things can happen to a textile item when it is being used.

First of all, physical forces can rub or tear at the fabric. We rub our elbows on a desk as we sit at it, or we may have an accident and catch the clothes on some wire, and anything like this can overcome the forces holding the fabric and the garment together and cause a break.

In addition, there are chemical forces at work. Of course, you don't normally dip your clothes in strong chemicals, but there are chemicals affecting your clothes every minute of the day – for example, perspiration, or the detergents they are washed in.

Finally, one of the most important things of all which causes fabrics to break down, we can't even see – ultra-violet light. This is part of the radiation which comes from the sun. But, unlike the light we see by, it is invisible to us. It is the same light which causes white people to go brown (and red) in the summer, and from which black people are protected because of pigments in their skin. But it attacks fibres and breaks down molecules. Have you ever wondered why a curtain eventually falls apart when it is hung at a window? It doesn't get any wear, except the occasional pull across. But if it is at a window facing the sunlight, the ultra-violet light gradually weakens it, and one day when you pull it it tears and a hole appears.

So the breakdown of textile items is very complicated, and no laboratory test has yet been produced which satisfactorily measures everything. The best tests are concerned with those physical forces such as rubbing and tearing, and these do give some guide to the length of time the fabric will last. They can also be used for measuring the strength of seams.

Of course, the fibres vary a lot in how strong they are. The strongest, which are particularly resistant to physical and chemical forces, are polyester and polyamide (nylon). Quite a long way below these in strength come wool, acrylic and silk, followed by cotton and, lower still, viscose, acetate and triacetate.

△ Martindale Tester – internationally accepted for abrasion in wear

8.4 Dimensional stability

If textiles shrink, they don't fit any more, which can cause a lot of trouble – collars can be too tight, chair covers won't fit the chair, curtains finish part-way up the window. Of course, fabrics can also extend, which may not be quite as bad but can make garments unwearable.

Why does this happen? Well, the reason is nearly always that the fabrics have not been properly finished. The fibres themselves don't shrink (with one exception), but fabrics do.

To test this, wash a square of the material, and measure it before and after washing.

The one exception to fibres not shrinking is wool, and even here it is not exactly the fibre itself that shrinks. However, when wool is wet any movement causes the fibres to tangle together, and the scales which are on the surface of the fibre lock the wool in this tangled position. In other words, it **felts**. This has always been a considerable problem with wool, which is why most washing instructions for wool items specify a gentle wash only, if at all. But the new finish now on the market, called Superwash and which can be applied to all wool knitwear, removes the problem of felting completely.

8.5 Changing shape

As we move about in our clothes, they change shape – they crease behind the knees and at elbows, they stretch at the knees, and the seat. If the clothes do not return to their original shape – that is, the creases fall out or the stretch recover – we do not like the appearance. This is especially true after washing, when a lot of creasing can occur, and if our textile items are creased we need to iron them, and that is a chore.

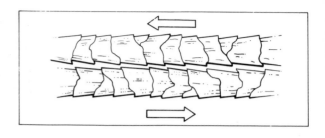

△ Locking of scales on wool – like a ratchet – fibre can move only as shown by arrows

▼ How textiles recover from creasing or
· stretching depends a lot on the fibre and
· the forces between the molecules. When
· a fibre is creased, for example, the inter-
· molecular forces are strained. When the
· force causing the creasing is released, if
· the inter-molecular forces are strong the
· creases will recover. For some fibres,
· such as wool and cotton, this ability is
· greatly affected by water, because water
· weakens the inter-molecular forces.
· Much of the time when we are wearing
· clothes, water is present, both in the air
· and from our own perspiration, and, of
· course, there is plenty of water around
▲ when we wash.

▷ The crease or pleat we want

The best fibres for crease recovery are polyester and polyamide (nylon). Acrylic is average. Wool, cotton, silk, viscose and acetate are all poor, especially when wet. Cotton and viscose can, however, be improved by a chemical finish called resin finishing. This gives cotton and viscose a minimum-iron finish – that is, the crease recovery is so good that they hardly need ironing, but – and this is a big but – the finish greatly weakens the fibres, and so minimum-iron cotton and viscose are very much weaker than they are in the natural state.

Although stretch recovery is important, for some items we need stretch – for example, in garments that fit close to the body, like tights and swimsuits. If these didn't stretch they would feel very uncomfortable.

Most of the stretch we need comes from the fabric. Knitted fabrics are more elastic than woven, and extra stretch comes from the yarn if it is textured. There is, however, one fibre on the market which is very stretchy in itself, and it is often added to garments which are close fitting and need a lot of stretch. That fibre is elastane (best known by the trade name Lycra).

This need for stretch explains the way some items are made – tights are made of knitted, textured nylon, T-shirts from knitted fabric, usually cotton, stretch jeans from cotton with elastane added, and swimsuits from nylon or cotton with elastane added.

Although we usually look for crease recovery, there is the sort of crease that we sometimes want to stay in our clothes. We usually call this sort of crease a pleat – in trouser legs and sometimes in skirts, for example. Any fabric can have a pleat put in it with an iron, but what matters is whether it stays in or not (is durable), especially when it is washed. The best fibres for this are polyester, polyamide (nylon) and triacetate.

Laboratory tests for shape retention usually involve taking a piece of fabric and washing it, and then looking at the amount of creasing which remains, to see how much ironing it needs. For pleat retention, the fabric is pleated and the wash test repeated. For stretch, and recovery from stretch, more complicated testing apparatus is used.

8.6 Drying

When textiles have been washed we need to dry them – and there are two good reasons why we like to be able to do this as quickly as possible.

1 It is more convenient – washing hanging about is a nuisance, and might get wet again if outdoors.

2 It may be cheaper – if we have to use heat to dry things (as in a tumble dryer) it costs money.

When fabrics get wet the water is held in three places:

1 in between the yarns of the fabric
2 in between the fibres in the yarns
3 in the fibres themselves

Water in 1 is easily removed; it just runs out when you hang up the item. Water in 2 is more difficult to remove, but it can be done by a spin dryer, for example, or by the action of the wind if it is hung on a line. In both 1 and 2, water is lost at the same rate for all fabrics, but in 3, the fibres themselves, the rate of water loss will vary.

Fibres differ in the amount of water they hold – some, such as polyester and polypropylene, hold virtually nothing, while others, such as wool, can hold a great deal. A fibre which holds a lot of water takes much longer to dry. It needs sunshine outdoors, or some form of heat, perhaps a tumble dryer, indoors. (Note that with wool, unless it has a Superwash finish to avoid felting, heat cannot be used, so wool garments take a very long time to dry.)

Fibres which hold a lot of water are called hydrophilic (water-loving). Those which hold little are called hydrophobic (water-hating). A table of the different fibres looks like this:

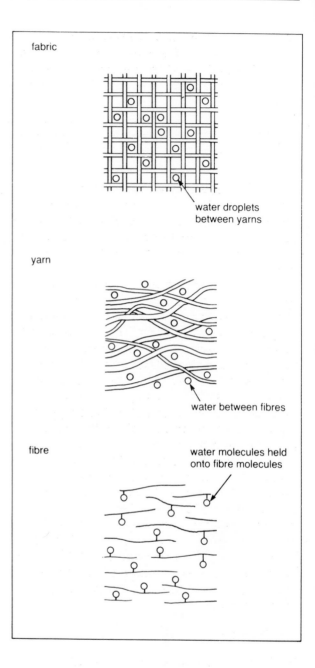

fabric

water droplets between yarns

yarn

water between fibres

fibre

water molecules held onto fibre molecules

wool viscose silk cotton acetate	} hydrophilic	increasingly water absorbing
triacetate nylon acrylic polyester polypropylene	} hydrophobic	increasingly drip-dry

▼ The amount of water a fibre holds
· depends on the fibre, the moisture in the
· air (humidity) and the temperature. At a
· given temperature and humidity we can
· say:
·
· $$\text{moisture content} = \frac{\text{weight of undried sample} - \text{weight of dried sample}}{\text{weight of undried sample}}$$
·

▲

When we see textiles labelled drip-dry, what is meant is that the fabric is made of mainly hydrophobic fibres which dry quickly (although you may think the name is rather silly, because everything drips and dries in the end).

But there is a problem – we want things to dry quickly, but we sometimes also want them to absorb water, and that means that they must be hydrophilic. Towels are a good example – polyester would not be much good for these. In addition, we all perspire, even when we are resting, but especially when we exercise. To stay comfortable, it helps if our clothes can absorb perspiration. So here we have the problem: the things that are the most difficult to dry are the most comfortable to wear (like cotton).

In practice, a lot (sometimes all) of the perspiration escapes through openings in our clothes (open necks, for example), or through the openings in the fabric itself – knits are more open (porous) than wovens. Therefore, it often does not matter too much which fibre we use, although if the fibre does absorb moisture it adds to the comfort of the garment.

8.7 Dyefast

We have seen how colour is put into textiles, but how do we make sure that it will stay there, and not come off on our bodies or on items in the wash? The answer is that we test – not just once, but for all the sorts of things which could happen and which could affect the dye.

First of all, in use or wear there are rubbing, perspiration and, in some ways worst of all, sunlight. Have you noticed how curtains fade when they are up at the window for a long time? Tests for all these things can be done in a laboratory using special apparatus. We don't have to wait for the sun to shine.

There are also tests for special cases. For example, chlorinated water is used to test swimsuit fabric in the sort of conditions it will have to put up with in the swimming pool.

Another thing we need to test for is fastness to washing, and there are two problems here:

1   We don't want the colour to change.
2   We don't want the dye to come off on to other things in the wash.

▼ We could just wash the item with a lot of
· other things to see what happened. But
· this is not very accurate, and is rather
· wasteful. Instead, in the laboratory a
· sample of fabric is washed in a machine
· (most laboratories use the same type),
· and a special test strip is sewn to it. This
· is called a multifibre test strip, and is
· made up of six different fibres (see
· photo). The washing conditions used first
· are those you would normally expect to
· wash the fabric at. When the sample
· comes out of the wash, it is examined to
· see if the colour has changed; then the
· multifibre test strip is looked at, to see if
· the colour has stained any of the fibres.
·   If the test is unsatisfactory, a number of
· things could happen then.

· 1   The fabric could be rejected and
·   perhaps sent for re-dyeing.
· 2   Another (lower temperature) wash
·   program could be tried.
· 3   The fabric could be given a 'dry clean
·   only' label.
· 4   If the colour change of the sample was
·   not too great, but the dye had stained
·   other fibres, it would obviously not be
·   safe to wash it with other items, so it
·   might be labelled 'wash separately'.

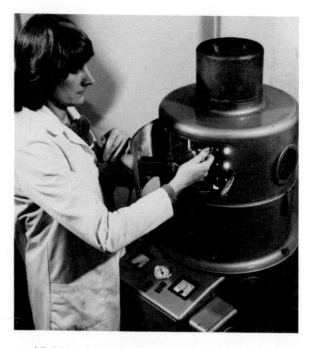

△ All this to imitate the sun – a Xenon arc lightfastness tester

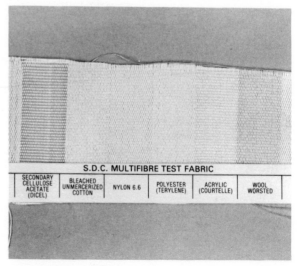

S.D.C. MULTIFIBRE TEST FABRIC					
SECONDARY CELLULOSE ACETATE (DICEL)	BLEACHED UNMERCERIZED COTTON	NYLON 6.6	POLYESTER (TERYLENE)	ACRYLIC (COURTELLE)	WOOL WORSTED

△ Multifibre test strip

- But how do we measure the change of
- colour, or staining? We can look at it, but
- each person would have their own ideas.
- So, in the laboratory, a change is
- measured with a special set of scales,
- called 'grey scales'. All these
- measurements must be carried out in
- standard conditions (that is, the same
- every time). You know that colours look
- different under different lights, so we use
▲ a standard light box.

Dye fastness is a problem, but it does not depend on which fibre is used. There are fast dyes in most colours for every fibre. The problem comes if the dyeing is not properly done. So, if the colours run and you have washed it correctly – blame the dyer!

△ Grey scales for assessing dye fastness values

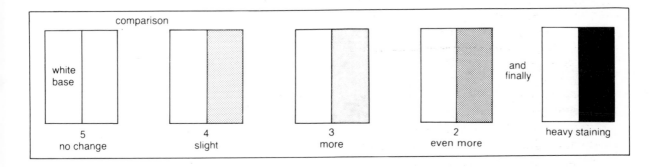

comparison				
white base				and finally
5 no change	4 slight	3 more	2 even more	heavy staining

△ A laboratory light box to give standard lighting conditions

8.8 **Cold, wind and rain**

Human beings are warm-blooded animals. Our bodies have a temperature of about 37°C which means that in most parts of the world the air temperature is lower than our body temperature, so we have to protect ourselves from the relative cold outside. At least, that is usually the case, but don't forget that in some countries, under some conditions (during the day in the desert, for example), we need to be protected from too much heat.

When it's cold, our bodies lose heat into the surroundings. If they lose it too quickly, in other words, we are not protected, we begin to shiver, which is the body's way of trying to keep us warm; but if the temperature difference is too great, the body gradually shuts down and in the end we die. This is what is meant by people dying of exposure, or as a result of hypothermia. We need protection because, although the body can make its own heat from the food we eat, it can do so only at a certain rate, and if we lose heat quicker than we make it, that's when the trouble starts. Of course, the bigger the temperature difference between ourselves and the outside, the more protection we need. If you were dropped into the Arctic, you wouldn't have long to live, unless you had some very good protective clothing.

▼ The body loses heat to the surroundings by the three methods of heat transfer, called conduction, convection and radiation. Protecting against all three of these becomes very important for people living or working in extremely cold climates, and for all of us on occasions – for example, if we go mountain walking in cold weather. In everyday life, protection against heat loss by conduction, and sometimes convection, is all we need, but even here, if we don't have that protection we feel chilly.

To protect ourselves from heat loss by conduction, we need to surround ourselves with something that acts as an insulator, that is, that does not conduct heat. Surprisingly perhaps, one of the best common insulators is air itself, but only if it can be kept still, or trapped in some way. And this is exactly what fabric does. A fabric consists of air trapped between the fibres, and so the thicker the fabric, the more air is trapped and the better insulator it is. That's why a thick overcoat keeps you warmer than a thin one. But the trouble with a traditional overcoat is that it can be very heavy, making it difficult to move about, so that it's harder for you to keep warm by your own body movements.

▽ The three ways we lose heat

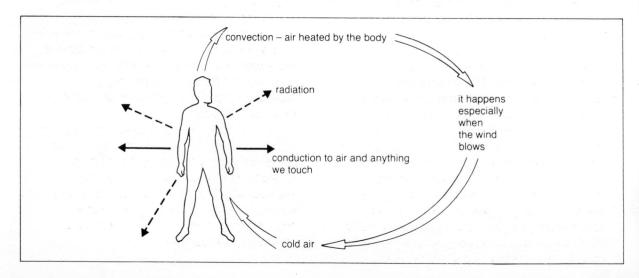

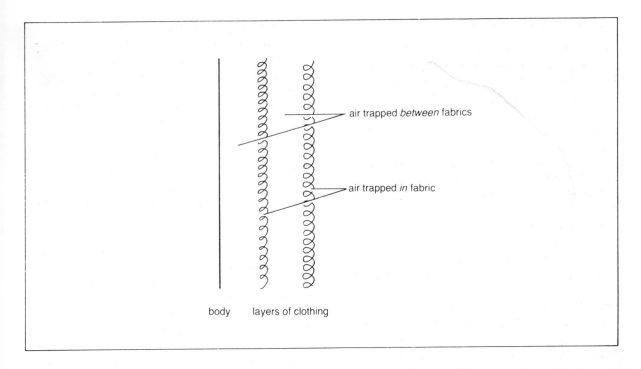

air trapped *between* fabrics

air trapped *in* fabric

body   layers of clothing

△ A textile is just air held together by fibres

One of the best ways to get thick insulation is to use a quilted fabric – fibre wadding with a woven fabric both outside and inside, held together by a few rows of stitching. Any quilted pattern can be used, although if too many stitches are put in they can form too many thin areas and so reduce the insulation. We use quilted fabrics for duvets and anoraks. Some fillings are feathers, others are fibre, usually polyester. The advantage of polyester is that it is washable.

For duvets, the insulation value is measured in togs. The higher the number, the better the insulation value, although it is not a good idea to have more than you need or you will get too hot. A tog value of 12–14 is about right for winter, dropping to 5 or 6 for summer.

You may have seen advertisements for 'thermal' clothes, especially underwear. What's so special about them? Some use fibres which have a low conductivity, but most are made from popular fibres such as polyester, wool and viscose. The fabrics are designed to trap as much air as possible, partly by brushing to give a raised surface. More air means better insulation, which in turn means more body heat retained.

One of the problems about insulating material is what happens when it gets wet – that is, if the air in the fabric is replaced by water. Water is a better conductor of heat than air, so the insulation value of clothes which get wet drops, because more heat is lost through the water. So clothing which is going to be used outdoors needs to be waterproofed if it is going to be effective in all conditions.

The only totally waterproof fabric is one which is coated with a plastic layer, as used, for example, on nylon fabrics in kagouls. Chemical finishes can be applied which give some resistance to water, but they do not keep out the heaviest rain and can sometimes be removed by cleaning.

But now comes another problem: the body is constantly giving off perspiration, and if we do not lose this perspiration, it turns into water on our skin, we feel uncomfortable and it soaks our clothing. If we are wearing a waterproof layer on the outside to keep the rain out, it may also keep the perspiration in, by the same principle. So we have a real problem, and one which has never been totally overcome, although, there are some special finishes which contain very tiny holes which will let virtually no water in but still allow the fabric to breathe (Gore-tex is an example). A simpler way, which helps a little, is to put holes in particular places in garments, for example under the arms, so that some air can circulate to remove perspiration, but rain cannot easily get in.

Heat loss by convection means heat loss when air is allowed to flow around the clothes. We can stop that simply by buttoning up at the neck, tightening up at the waist, buttoning up cuffs etc., but that only works if the wind is not blowing, because if it is and it can blow through our clothes, it will remove heat from our bodies and we get what is often called the 'chill factor' of the wind. We get this problem particularly with knitted fabrics. A thick sweater can keep you very warm as long as the wind does not blow, but when it does it goes straight through. So, for windy conditions, once again we need a fabric which the wind can't go through – something like a tightly-woven nylon kagoul, or a tightly-woven polyester/cotton or cotton fabric, such as the outer layer of an anorak.

Finally, heat loss may be by radiation. Anything hot radiates (gives out) heat; you can feel this if you put your hand near the fire, without touching it. This source of heat loss is very important in cold conditions, so how can we stop this heat getting away from our bodies? The way to do it is to reflect the heat back to the body with a shiny surface, such as aluminium. Clothing used for extreme cold has aluminium foil built into it, which reflects the heat back to the body, just like the survival bags that people carry with them for hill-climbing expeditions.

Keeping warm is quite complicated. We need thick clothes, and we also need clothes that the wind and rain can't penetrate if we are going outdoors. One of the best ways of doing this while still allowing yourself to be free to move around is to build up layers of clothing, with the outer one being wind- and rainproof. Remember that not only do you have the thickness of the fabrics themselves, but also the air trapped in between the fabrics.

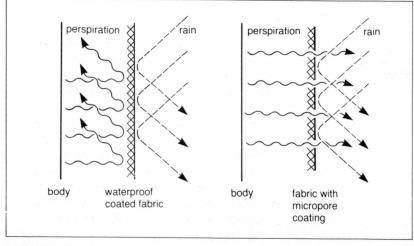

△ Beating the wet

△ Don't forget shiny side inside!

8.9 Fire

Fire is a terrible hazard, and it would be comforting to think, if we were ever in a dangerous situation, that our clothes would protect us from it. Unfortunately, they cannot protect us completely, because very few fibres are totally resistant to fire. Those that are, such as asbestos and glass, are not the sort you would want to wear.

All the commonly used fibres will burn if they come into contact with fire. They do, however, vary in terms of what happens when they are removed from the fire – whether they go on burning or go out, and that could be very important in saving lives.

△ Make sure it doesn't happen to you!

The best fibre for going out immediately is modacrylic, which is why it is used for dressing-gowns and rugs which may go near an open fire. Wool and silk are also good; they will go out almost immediately. Polyester and polyamide (nylon) may continue burning for a while, but usually only slowly, and although they drop molten plastic, which can be very painful, they go out fairly quickly. Acrylic, cotton and viscose, however, go on burning – cotton and viscose very fast indeed. It is possible to put fire-resisting finishes on to fibres, particularly cotton and viscose (for example, Proban finish), but they are not very popular for everyday use (although they are used in industry) because they tend to make the fabric stiff and can be damaged if not washed under the correct conditions. They can also be expensive.

We can use the burning properties of fibres as a way of identifying them. Take a few fibres from a piece of fabric, or use a *small* (1 × 1 cm) square, and holding it in a pair of tweezers or tongs, bring the sample slowly towards a flame (a bunsen burner or a candle) until it starts to burn. Then remove it, and see what happens.

Fibre	Flame test
Cotton	Burns rapidly with a clear flame, leaving a powdery ash smelling of burnt paper
Linen	Like cotton
Viscose	Like cotton, but ash may be black and slightly sticky
Wool and silk	Quickly goes out, smells like burnt hair
Nylon and polyester	Burns slowly, dropping molten polymer and with smoky flame; usually goes out leaving hard beads
Acrylic	Burns with smoky flame and dropping molten polymer
Modacrylic	Goes out immediately

To avoid some of the worst types of fire, the law forbids the use of cotton and viscose fabric on nightdresses and party dresses for children. But the sad fact is that none of the fibres we use commonly can give us total protection, although some are safer to wear than others because they do at least go out when the source of fire is removed. There is a particular danger area in furniture with fabric covers. A carelessly dropped cigarette can smoulder, and set fire not only to the cover but also to the foam underneath giving the extra danger of fumes. Foams that give off poisonous fumes when burning have now been banned, but older furniture may contain them, and great care must be taken.

It is only by taking great care that we can really deal with the problem of fire. Don't allow your clothes or household textiles to catch fire in the first place. Open fires are dangerous unless properly guarded. Cigarettes are not only dangerous to health, they are also a fire hazard. Oil heaters and electric fires that are not properly guarded can be lethal. *Never* let children play with matches.

For those who fight fires or who work in dangerous conditions near fire, special

clothes are available – but they are hardly fashionable!

△ Don't expect your clothes to save you

8.10 **Which is best?**

If we think about the performance properties we look for, which fibre comes out best? The answer is: none – all the time.

Polyester and polyamide are best for strength and easy care, but not for comfort (absorbing perspiration).

Cotton wins for comfort, but not for quick drying or fire resistance.

Wool is good (but not the best) for durability, but not for washing and drying.

So, when we are designing a particular item we need to decide which properties are the most important, and choose the fibre (as well as the fabric structure and finish) which will best do the job. Sometimes, of course, we may decide that a blend is the best all round. This is often the answer, which is why blends are so popular.

8.11 **What are your rights?**

In the past twenty years, new laws have improved the position of the consumer (customer) in the battle against people who sell shoddy or unsafe goods, or who trade dishonestly, although some people believe that the law is still not strict enough.

There are fewer laws which relate to textiles than for some other products, for example food, but let's see what protection there is.

We have already seen (in Chapter 2) that a retailer must tell you what fibres a textile item is made from, but that is all he must tell you. There does not have to be a label for cleaning instructions, or country of origin (where the item was made). However, if these things are mentioned or any other thing is stated about the item, the Trade Descriptions Act says that it must be true. So a trader who tells you (verbally or on a label) that your sweater was made in the UK, when in fact it was made somewhere else, can be prosecuted. This also applies to someone who sells you second-hand goods claiming they are new.

There is only one performance property clearly mentioned in a regulation, and that is fire resistance. As we have seen in this chapter, cotton and viscose cannot be used for children's nightdresses or party clothes. In addition, furniture which will burn if a cigarette or matches are dropped on it must have a warning label attached.

Other performance properties are partly covered by the Sale of Goods Act, which says that items must be of 'merchantable quality'. This means that if you are sold an item, such as a shirt, it must perform as you would reasonably expect a shirt to perform. For example, it must not rapidly fall apart, and you must be able to wash it.

A trader can also be prosecuted if an item sold is dangerous and injures you. Fortunately, textile fabrics don't have the same problems as, say, electrical goods, but sometimes trimmings can be dangerous (like fasteners fitted into a garment by spikes that are not sealed off). New laws are likely to make it an offence to offer for sale any items which could be dangerous.

If you do have a problem with any item, take or send it back to the retailer and complain, or if it is serious, go to your local Trading Standards Office.

One thing which often happens to textile items is that they are sold in 'sales'. The

△ You have been warned!

law says that before a trader can state that an item has been reduced, it must have been on sale at the old price for a continuous period of 28 days in the past 6 months. Some store chains get round this by having the item on sale at the 'normal' price in one of their shops (often in a remote part of the country), and then offering it for sale everywhere showing a big reduction; or a store may buy in goods 28 days before the 'sales', and put them on sale at a ridiculously high price in order to show a big reduction when the 'sale' comes.

The lesson from this is that the only sure bargain reduction is one where you have seen the item on sale at the old price for some time (more than a month) before the 'sales'.

In the end, consumer rights and the law are important, but you can help yourself a great deal if you know something about textiles and what to look out for – this can help to save you from buying faulty goods in the first place.

Summary

Although textile items, especially for clothes and the home, need to look good, they must stand up to wear and use (perform) to the standard we want.

Some of the most important properties are how long the item lasts, whether it will keep its size (especially on washing), whether it will remain creased after wear and cleaning, whether the colours are fast, and how quickly it dries or absorbs moisture. We also need to know whether our clothes will keep us warm.

All these properties could be measured by wearing and using textiles, but this is not very practical, so instead, laboratory tests are generally used.

The different fibres have different performance properties. Polyester and nylon are the strongest, generally give the best creasing performance, and needing minimum ironing after washing, but are poor at absorbing moisture and so, although quick drying, are less comfortable to wear than wool or cotton.

Wool has a shrinkage problem (felting) related to the fibre itself.

Cotton and viscose burn considerably, even when the source of fire is removed.

Dye fastness does not depend on the fibres, but on the method of dyeing.

Insulation depends on fabric and garment structure rather than on fibre, thick windproof items giving the greatest protection.

The fact that no fibre is ideal in all performance terms is one of the reasons why blends are popular.

The consumer has some protection from poor textile items, but much less than for food. The only performance property definitely referred to in any regulation is flame resistance – cotton and viscose fabrics cannot be used for certain children's wear.

Questions

1 Are these statements true or false?

   a Hydrophobic means a fibre absorbs a lot of water.
   b A dimensionally stable fabric does not shrink.
   c Polyester has better crease recovery than viscose.
   d Modacrylic fibres do not burn.
   e Water is a better insulator than air.

2 Complete the following:

   a Curtains lose most of their strength because of the effect of _____.
   b When wool is washed, the _____ on the fibres cause it to felt.
▼ c A _____ test strip is used to see if dye comes off on to other fibres in the wash.
· d The insulation value of duvets is
▲   measured in _____.
   e The _____ _____ Act says that any label on a garment must be correct.

3 The properties required of a fabric will vary according to its use. From the list given below, state four properties you would want in each item.

a underwear
b children's wear
c sports wear
d bedlinen

The properties to choose from are: cool, hard wearing, crease shedding, colour fast, anti-static, absorbent, elastic, showerproof, non-irritant, quick drying, warm, shrink resistant, stain resistant.

4 List four textile items where stretch is an important property.

5 a What is meant by flame retardant?
  b Suggest four items in the home which should be flame retardant.

6 a What is meant by minimum iron?
  b Name one fabric with such a property.
  c Suggest three uses for such a fabric.

7 Which test is more efficient, and why – a wearer trial or a laboratory test?

8 a What is a drip-dry fabric? Explain the words hydrophilic and hydrophobic.
  b In the following pairs, which would you expect to dry first?

    (i)   silk and polyester
    (ii)   wool and cotton
    (iii) nylon and viscose
    (iv)   triacetate and acrylic
    (v)   resin-treated cotton and natural cotton

9 a What specific laws are there regarding children's nightwear?
  b Suggest two fabrics which should not be used, and explain why.

10 a List the details you would expect to find on a garment you might purchase.
   b What steps would you take if a tracksuit you purchased split a seam after wearing and washing once?

Design brief

You have been asked to submit designs to a local health authority for clothes for an old people's home, for both men and women.

The old people can get about, but rarely go out except into the gardens in summer.

The local authority does not want to produce a uniform, but the clothes should be easily produced on a large scale to keep down costs.

Select five outerwear or bedwear items, and produce a full design specification for each. This should include:

1 a sketch of the garment showing style and any features, including things such as pockets and method of fastening

2 a list of performance properties which will be important for the fabric and the garment

3 some suggested fabrics, and the fibres they are made from, for the main parts of the clothes

4 any special notes regarding the trimmings to be used

9

How much?

When you buy a textile item, the chances are you will not buy it from the person or firm who made it; you will buy it from someone whose business is concerned with making goods available to the public – this business is called **retailing and distributing**.

There are several types of retailer, the most common being a shop or store (now quickly think of some more) – but before we get into too much detail, let's look at the money side.

9.1 Totting up the cost

Let's suppose you bought a pair of trousers for £18. The retailer has bought those trousers from a manufacturer, perhaps for £10, and the £8 added on is the retailer's **mark-up**.

▼ This mark-up is often talked about in
· the trade as a percentage, so try to work
· out the mark-up, first as a percentage of
· the cost price (what the retailer paid the
· manufacturer) and then as a percentage
· of the selling price (what the retailer sold
· it to you for).
·   Let's call the price you pay (what the
· retailer sells it for) the Selling Price, and
· the price the retailer pays (what the
· manufacturer sells it for) the Cost Price.
·
· So Mark-up = Selling Price − Cost Price
·
· as a percentage of Selling Price =
·
· $\dfrac{\text{Mark-up}}{\text{Selling Price}} \times 100$
·
· as a percentage of Cost Price =
·
· $\dfrac{\text{Mark-up}}{\text{Cost Price}} \times 100$

· The percentage is, therefore, different
· depending on how you calculate it; so if
· somebody ever quotes you a mark-up,
· make sure you know which way they have
· calculated it. In this book we will always
▲ use Cost Price as the base.

Many people refer to the mark-up as the retailer's **profit**, but this is not really correct. Why? Well, out of the mark-up the retailer has to pay all the expenses of running the business (these are sometimes called the overheads). These vary with the type of retailer, but can include:

1 Wages and salaries – the manager, the sales assistants, the cleaners.
2 Cost of the place where business is carried out – rent, mortgage, rates.
3 Heating and lighting – gas, electricity, oil, coal.
4 Advertising – ads in the paper, local radio, TV, catalogues.
5 Shopfittings – counters, display stands, fitting rooms, carpets.

Add all these up and they equal **expenses**, so to get the actual profit:

Mark-up − expenses = profit

And it is this profit which goes to the owners of the business.

115

So, how does a shop make a profit? It puts a big enough mark-up on everything it sells to cover the expenses, with a bit to spare. For example, suppose one week a shop sold 1000 items and made £5 mark-up on each one; it would have made £5000 total mark-up. If expenses for that week were £4000, everyone would be happy. But suppose the next week it sold only 500 items, and expenses stayed the same. It is easy to see that the total money coming in would not be enough to cover the expenses, and there would be a **loss** – and if that went on the retailer would eventually go **bankrupt** and have to close down. Think of some shops in your area that have had to do that.

▼ To see how sales and mark-up have to balance against expenses, let's look at a more detailed problem:

Two shops, Mighty Modes and Trendy Textiles, are in business in the same town. They have the following expenses per week:

	Mighty Modes	Trendy Textiles
Rent and rates on shop	£500	£500
Loan from bank for fittings	50	10
Wages	400	200
Heating and lighting	50	40
Advertising	200	50
	£1200	£800

Both have a mark-up of 100% on cost price.

Business is difficult for everyone, but this week Mighty Modes' advertising seems to have attracted a number of people and they sold £2000 worth of textile goods. Trendy Textiles sold £1700 worth.

So are they making a profit? What do you think?

If both have mark-ups of 100% then the first thing we need to know is what the goods they sold actually cost them – then we will know their mark-up in money.

From our equation (page 115):

percentage

$$M.U. = \frac{S.P. - C.P.}{C.P.} \times 100$$

for Mighty Modes

$$100 = \frac{2000 - C.P.}{C.P.} \times 100$$

$$C.P. = 2000 - C.P.$$
$$2C.P. = 2000$$

C.P. = 1000	Mark-up = £1000

and for Trendy Textiles

C.P. = £850	Mark-up = £850

– which is obvious, since a mark-up of 100% on cost price means we double the cost price to get the selling price.

So who is making a profit?

Mighty Modes   Profit = £1000 − 1200 = £200 *LOSS*
Trendy Textiles   Profit = £850 − 800 = £50

  Now let's work it out for the following week if Mighty Modes' sales are £2200 and Trendy Textiles' £1800:

Mighty Modes   Profit = £1100 − 1200 = £100 *LOSS*
Trendy Textiles   Profit = £900 − 800 = £100

Mighty Modes is still in trouble, and if it goes on like this they could well have to close.

So what could Mighty Modes do?

The immediate thought is to cut expenses:

– employ fewer assistants and cut the wages bill
– advertise less

But it might then attract fewer people

Is there another way?

What about these:

– increase the mark-up
– sell more

Suppose it charged more for everything it sold – it would make more mark-up, so covering its expenses – but would it happen? Might not people think everything was too expensive, and shop elsewhere?

What about the second way? How could it sell more?

- Well, we don't know a lot about Mighty Modes, but suppose it
- just wasn't offering the right sort of goods for many of the
- people who came into the shop. You know, the sort of shop
- that never has quite the things you are looking for. If it bought
- more of the right things from the manufacturers it might sell
- more of them.

. We don't know which would work – but you can see that it is
▲ not all that easy to be a retailer.

How does a retailer decide what mark-up to put on the items they sell? This is based first of all on the size of the expenses (or overheads) – the bigger they are, the higher will have to be the mark-up. So the expenses are very important to you, the customer, because they decide how much you pay.

Now we can look in more detail at other sorts of retailing and distribution outlets – and at the same time see how their expenses vary and, therefore, how much you will have to pay.

9.2 **Shops and stalls**

From Harrods to a market stall, from Marks and Spencer with over 200 stores to the handicraft shop in the village, there are thousands of places where textiles are sold.

But they differ a lot. They differ in what is offered to you – the customer – and the sorts of facilities the shop provides.

Because of the variety, it is difficult to divide them up into groups (that is, attempt some classification), but here is a list of the different types of places that sell textiles – and most important, something about them so that we can get an idea of what their expenses are and so how much mark-up they need to charge.

As you go through, try to put some names to the types in your area, and then check these against the table on page 127.

Anytown Shopping Centre

Department stores

- Big stores in main streets or shopping centres – may be part of a Group.

- Sell a wide range of goods, including textiles, in 'departments'.

- Offer a wide choice with lots of different brand names.

- Usually 'plushy' surroundings with plenty of displays.

- Usually a lot of assistants.

- Big 'sales' – widely advertised.

Variety chain stores

- Generally big stores in the main street or shopping centre.

- Always in a group, with branches selling virtually the same items all over the country.

- Sell a variety of goods, including textiles, but generally a fairly limited selection – usually own brand name only.

- Fairly plain surroundings.

- Assistants generally only at checkouts.

- Do not often advertise.

Specialist chain stores or multiples

- Different size stores in main street or shopping centre – part of a group, with branches all over the country.

- Sell textile items only, and generally only certain types, for example children's wear.

- Fairly good choice, often own brand name only.

- Surroundings vary, some may be fairly 'plushy'.

- Number of assistants varies, some may offer specialist advice.

Supermarkets

- Large stores either just off or in main shopping area.

- Specialize in food, but some textiles sold as well.

- Basic items only, such as tights.

- Plain surroundings.

- Assistants only at checkouts.

Hypermarkets

- Very large supermarkets, usually in out-of-town area.

- Bigger range of goods which includes more textiles.

Market stalls

- Either in street or in special market halls.

- Very basic facilities.

- Range very limited, often sell 'seconds'.

- One or two persons on stall only.

Market stallholders cannot generally buy direct from manufacturers because they are too small, so they buy from **wholesalers**, often working from cash and carry warehouses. Wholesalers hold stocks of goods from a number of manufacturers. This means an extra person in the middle between the manufacturer and the retailer, and this 'middleman' has to make a profit which, of course, goes on to the price you pay.

Independents

- A single shop, or maybe one or two branches in the area.

- May be in main shopping area, local shopping area, side street or village.

- May specialize.

- Not big enough to have own brand name, may buy from wholesalers.

- May be 'factory shop' attached to and run by a manufacturer, often as a means of getting rid of 'seconds'.

- Surroundings vary – some very plushy some very plain.

- Some special names:
    Boutique – trendy clothes for men and women, often unisex
    Outfitter – more traditional men's and boys' wear
    Couture – expensive, exclusive women's clothes

Now, how much do you pay? It depends on the shop's expenses. Obviously, a main shopping area, plushy surroundings, lots of assistants, and big selection costs money. But you might want those things, and be prepared to pay for them.

   But remember something else (and the problem at the end of this chapter shows this), the more successful a shop is – that is, the more it offers what a lot of people want – the more it sells, and therefore the more mark-up it collects to cover its expenses. So it can then afford to keep prices down, even though it may be paying a lot of rent and rates for being in a main shopping area.

So let's look at the various types of shop or stall and see what we come up with for mark-up.

Highest (sometimes over 200% on cost price) – very trendy, exclusive boutiques and couture shops.

Middle (a little over 100% on cost price) – department stores, average independents, some specialist chains, some market stalls.

Lowest (about 70% on cost price) – variety chain stores, most specialist chains, some market stalls, super- and hypermarkets.

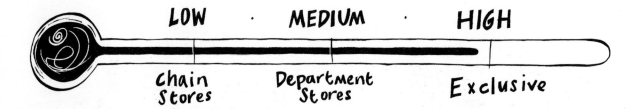

LOW · MEDIUM · HIGH

Chain Stores Department Stores Exclusive

9.3 Catalogues

A lot of people hate shopping, or rather they dislike the fuss of getting to the shops, parking the car or getting on crowded buses, and so on. Or maybe they are disabled, and find shopping particularly difficult. So what would be a good system for them? – Having a 'shop' in their home, and having the goods they have chosen delivered to the door.

At its simplest, an advertisement in a paper or a journal is enough. You look at a picture of the item, decide you like the look of it, and send off the money. This is generally a safe method of shopping because the newspaper owners provide protection against dishonest traders.

But the most popular shopping-at-home system in the UK is mail-order catalogue. Think of some you know, and check with the table at the end of the chapter.

You may know the way this works. If you

are over eighteen, you can become an agent of the company. You send off for a catalogue. There are usually two each year. You can buy from this catalogue yourself, or show it to friends and neighbours and get them to buy from it. If you do this, you get commission from the company (usually 10% of what is bought). You order from the company and the goods are delivered to your door.

There is one other important thing to note – most mail order companies let you pay after you have got the goods on a weekly or monthly basis over periods up to a year (in other words, you get credit). It's a convenient system, but let's see how it compares with shops on cost.

Well, catalogues don't need expensive main shopping area sites – they can have warehouses in cheaper areas to store their goods.

However, they do have to pay for the big, glossy catalogue, plus all the delivery costs (both ways if you send the goods back).

They don't have assistants, but they do need people in the warehouse – and they do have to pay you, as the agent.

Finally, they have to finance the credit they give you – because they will have to pay the manufacturer long before you have paid them all you owe.

So, what do you think on balance – what sort of mark-up? Well, it's round about department store level. But remember, to balance the cost you can have the convenience of shopping in your own home.

Some of the newer mail order catalogues do not work by agency and offer more limited credit, some even charge for the catalogue.

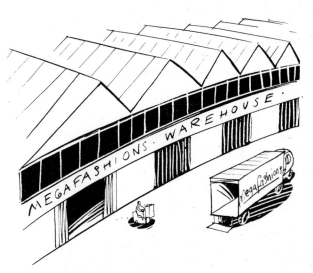

9.4 Party Plan

Most people like parties and meeting their friends, so someone came up with the idea of organizing parties at which you sell goods.

In the UK, this started with plastic containers for the kitchen, but has gone on to include textiles (see table at the end of the chapter).

You organize a party (any sort) with the help of an 'organizer' from the company. At the party you show samples of the goods (model them if you like) and take orders. The orders are delivered by the company later. You get a commission on what is sold (usually 10%).

If you think about it, party plan is a bit like mail order, and the expenses are about the same. There may not be a glossy catalogue, but the firm has to pay for the organizer.

So, mark-up here is about the same as mail order – but you don't have to go shopping and you may like the excuse for a party.

9.5 Do-it-yourself

'A sewing machine, a sewing machine, a girl's best friend' – so went the old song. But is it true today? Is it worthwhile for a boy or girl to make their own clothes, or perhaps get them made for them by a relative or friend?

This chapter is about cost, so we will look at it from that point of view, although of course, if you enjoy making your own clothes and you do not mind the time it takes or (within reason) the cost, it will be worthwhile, like any other leisure or social activity.

So let's look at the cost. To start with, most people will not want (or have the skill) to spin their own yarn or make their own fabric. So that's cost number one.

When you buy the knitting yarn or the fabric, you come across the first problem. The price you pay is much more than a manufacturer would pay. You buy knitting yarn (don't call it 'wool', because not all knitting yarn is made from wool) or fabric from a shop, often a department store, and they charge high mark-ups. The only way you could save here is if you live near a fabric maker who has a factory shop, or by buying from a market stall – but can you always get what you want, and what is the standard?

Then you have to buy the trimmings – at high mark-up (the zip that costs you £1 would probably cost a garment maker less than 40p).

Then there's the pattern.

And finally, there is one more thing you should add – the cost of the machines you need. If you have to buy a sewing or knitting machine and you don't use it that often, it makes a lot of difference to the *real* cost of what you make (think about it).

Of course, clothes are all about looking

good – can you make the item look as good as a good shop garment?

Add it all up, and it is doubtful whether, for *everyday* clothing, it's worth making it yourself, as against the sort of value you get in the lower mark-up areas.

So is it ever? Well, there are some items – special items – perhaps for special occasions, that are very expensive to buy because they are only sold in shops with high or very high mark-ups. These include garments for when you want to look different – or exclusive. Think of some occasions or items – what about weddings, or special designer-knit sweaters?

If you have the skill – and the time – you can save. You might even sell a few and make some mark-up yourself – but then you would be in the textile retail business.

9.6 How do you get value for money?

Very few people have enough money for everything they want, so most people have to be careful with their money. They have to 'shop around'. But how do we ensure that we get good value?

Some people say 'you get what you pay for' – but is it true? We have seen in our look at retailers that they vary a lot in the mark-up they put on. So you might think that going to a retailer with the lowest mark-up would be the first step to good value. Obviously, it's a start, but it is not the whole answer. Why?

Remember, the retailer did not make the textile item you buy. A few big retailers, such as the chain stores, have a big influence on what manufacturers produce (some even own their own factories), but if a retailer buys a poor garment from a manufacturer it is hardly likely to be good value, even with the lowest mark-up. One way to reduce the risk here is to look for retailers who carry out tests on the textiles they buy – the big chain stores, most mail-order companies and some department stores do this.

But let's ask ourselves another question. What do we mean by 'good value'?

We have seen that people buy textiles for a number of reasons. Sometimes they are very concerned about how an item will wear and wash, but more often than not it is the 'look' they are after, what sort of image it gives them, both for clothes and household items.

To get that fashion look you may be willing to pay a lot, and you may have to go to the more trendy or exclusive shops and pay a higher mark-up to get it. And that, you might well feel, is good value. But, having done that, there is no reason why you should not get a reasonable standard of wear. Unfortunately, expensive fashion items are not always the best made and so, for all sorts of textile items, here are a few guidelines to help you reduce the risk of getting a poorly manufactured item:

1   Always look for the fibre content label – it should be there by law. If it is not, reject the item and complain to the manager or to the local Trading Standards office.

2   Look at the fibre content. If you want something to be particularly hard wearing but the item is made from a fibre which you know is weak, such as viscose, reject it.

3   Look for the cleaning instructions. Even though they are not required by law, if they are not there, reject the item.

4   Compare the fibre label and the cleaning instructions. If they do not 'add up', be very suspicious. For example, you know that polyester is an easily washable fibre. If the item contains 50% or more polyester and is marked 'dry clean only' or 'hand-wash', then the chances are that the fabric or make up is poor in some way.

5   Look again at the care label. If it says 'wash separately', it probably means that the dye will run, so if it is something that you would normally want to wash with other things, reject it.

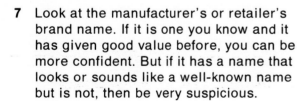

6   Look at the trimmings, especially linings. If they are made from fibres with a poorer performance than the main fabric, reject the item.

7   Look at the manufacturer's or retailer's brand name. If it is one you know and it has given good value before, you can be more confident. But if it has a name that looks or sounds like a well-known name but is not, then be very suspicious.

Finally, if you buy a textile item which does not perform to what you feel is a reasonable standard – *take it back and complain*. Remember, you have rights, which are outlined in Chapter 8. If you are reasonable but the retailer is not, that's a very good reason for not shopping there again.

Table of retailers

Department stores	House of Fraser (includes Harrods, D. H. Evan, Army & Navy, Kendal Milne, Binns, Dingles, Rackhams, Howells, Frasers) Debenhams (includes Harvey Nichols) Selfridges Allders
Variety chain stores	Marks & Spencer, BHS, Woolworths, Littlewoods, Boots, Co-op
Specialist chain stores	C. & A., Mothercare, Next, Olympus, Burtons, Fosters, Dorothy Perkins, Top Shop
Supermarkets	Tesco, Sainsburys, Asda, International, Safeway, Gateway
Hypermarkets	Asda, Carrefour, Tesco, Woolco, Supasaver
Market stalls	all over the country; the most famous is Petticoat Lane (Middlesex Street, London)
Mail order (agency)	G.U.S. Group (Great Universal Stores, Kays) Littlewoods Group (John Craig, Janet Fraser, John Moores, Burlington, Brian Mills) Freemans Grattons
Party plan	Pippa Dee

Summary

Retailers and distributors make textile items available to the general public, but they do not all have shops; some sell through catalogues, by party plan or by advertisements in papers. Shops vary from small independents to big department stores with famous names.

Retailers have to make a profit to stay in business. They do this by adding a mark-up to the cost of the goods they buy from manufacturers. This mark-up aims to cover their expenses and to leave a profit. The amount of mark-up varies between retailers because their expenses vary. You pay more for exclusivity and luxury surroundings.

Questions

1 Are these statements true or false?

a A retailer manufactures textile items for sale to the public.
b Some retailers do not have shops.
c The retailers' mark-up goes back to them as profit.
d Retailers add on mark-up only to cover their expenses.
e The bigger the company, the higher the percentage mark-up it adds on.

2 Fill in the blanks.

a _____ chain stores sell a number of different things, including textiles.
b _____ stores offer a wide variety and have high overheads.

c One method of shopping at home is to send for a _____ catalogue.

d The pattern, the material and the _____ are all part of the cost of making at home.

e With the help of the retailer's organizer, you can have a _____ and sell at home.

3 Give three reasons why you think most clothes are bought ready made rather than made at home.

4 Put the following in order of increasing mark-up: boutique, variety chain store, party plan.

5 You like the look of three textile items and they are all about the same price. The labels in them are as follows:

| 67/33 polyester/cotton
lining: viscose
hand wash separately | 67/33 polyester/cotton
lining: nylon
machine wash at 50°C | polyester/cotton
this garment is made
to the highest standards
dry clean only |

Which do you think is likely to be the best buy?

▼ 6 Three shops are in competition in our town –FABULOUS FASHIONS, UNSEX SWINGERS, and BEST SHOP BOUTIQUE.
Each shop has a slogan:

Fabulous Fashions – *Nobody, but nobody, is cheaper*

Unisex Swingers – *The trendiest in town*

Best Shop Boutique – *We give you the jet-set image*

Fabulous Fashions is the biggest shop, but there is not much in the way of fixtures and fittings, and few assistants. Rails of garments spill out on to the pavement, sometimes leading to complaints by the local authority. They often hold sales, which are advertised.

Unisex Swingers is a medium-sized shop. The owners spend quite a lot on fixtures and fittings, which they keep changing. Their manageress writes a column in the local paper on fashion where she gets in some plugs for the shop, and they also spend a fair bit on advertising new lines. They often have lines which don't make it, so they have to be sold off cheaply. They have a large stock, and the shop is sometimes a bit over-crowded.

Best Shop Boutique spent a lot of money to begin with on fixtures and fittings, to give a very expensive look to the shop. It has two sales only during the year, which are advertised. It is not a big shop, but there are several assistants who give personal attention and wear some of the items on sale.

The expenses of the shops look like this: (all £ per week):

	F.F.	U.S.	B.B.
Rent, rates etc.	1800	1200	600
Fixtures & fittings	90	210	150
Wages	750	600	900
Heat and light	150	120	150
Advertising	900	600	150
Mark-up on cost price	75%	100%*	150%

*because of mark downs, $\frac{1}{4}$ of all sales at 0%

The sales for the past four weeks are as follows: (all £ per week)

	F.F.	U.S.	B.B.
Week 1	10,500	6000	6000
Week 2	7,875	3600	3000
Week 3	11,550	7200	6750
Week 4	8,025	4800	4500

a (i) What are the expenses for each shop per week?
  (ii) Why do you think Fabulous Fashions' are the highest?
b (i) What is the mark-up of each shop per week?
  (ii) What is the total mark-up for each shop for the 4-week period?
  (iii) Who appears to be doing best?
c (i) Work out the profit for each shop.
  (ii) One shop is making a loss – explain why this is.
  (iii) What do you think they could do to make a profit?
d (i) Work out the percentage profit on sales.
    $\frac{\text{Profit}}{\text{Sales}} \times 100$
  (ii) One shop is making a much higher profit than the others. Why do you think this is?
e Week 2 wasn't good for anybody. List three reasons why this could be.

Here are some things to do which will help in your understanding of retailing and in answering the design brief:

1 Go to your local shopping centre or main shopping area and make a list of shops selling textile items. Put them into the various categories.

2 Think especially about shops in your area which have newly opened or recently closed. If they have closed, have you any idea why?

3 Think of all the items you can that are used to display textiles in stores. Go and check to see if you have forgotten any. Compare what is used in different types of stores.

4 Imagine that you have just been made manager of a department store. Think of all the textile departments you might have, and think of a way of promoting or publicizing them in the store – you might get some famous people to come to the store, for example. Decide on one method for each department.

5 Think of some textile brand names belonging to retailers, and then some belonging to manufacturers. Make a list, and then check in stores to see what you might have missed.

6 Imagine that you are a small garment manufacturer. Design a newspaper advertisement to sell a textile item that you make.

7 Bring in some mail-order catalogues. Try to find some items which are the same, or nearly the same, as those sold in shops. Compare the prices. (As a start, try men's formal shirts, women's stockings and tights, sheets and duvet covers.)

8 You are running a party to sell textiles. Work out what it will cost and how much you would have to sell to make a profit. (You will need to decide what items you are selling and how much you can expect to sell to each person.)

9 Design yourself a garment for a special occasion, or select one from a pattern book. Work out the cost of making it yourself (don't forget to include everything), and compare that with a ready-made item as similar as possible to it (possibly from a catalogue).

10 Select an everyday garment, and compare the cost of making it yourself with a similar item from a chain store.

Design brief

Two friends have decided to put their redundancy money together and sell clothes and household items which they are going to make themselves, or get local people to make in their homes.

The problem is that they do not know which retail method to use. Should they open a shop, sell by newspaper advertisements, issue a small catalogue, or perhaps do a party plan in the area?

They have asked your advice, so you must decide on one retail method and produce a plan for them of what they will need to do.

First, explain briefly why you have chosen that particular method, then:

1 Suggest a name for their retail operation.

2 Outline the sorts of textile items they are going to sell – men's, women's children's, unisex, household, etc.

3 Show the layout of their shop (if any), giving details of fixtures and fittings, or design advertisements and/or catalogue, if required.

4 Decide whether they will need extra staff or can manage it all themselves. Organize the work of the retail organization between the two friends and any staff they may need.

5 Make an estimate, based on everything you think is important, of what sort of mark-up they will have to apply to the textile items they sell.

10
What is designing?

In the past nine chapters we have looked at textiles. We have seen what a wide range of things the term textiles covers, and what an enormous part of our everyday lives textiles are involved in.

We have also seen that to understand and use textiles, you need certain skills. These may be artistic (in creating style, colour and fashion), or they may be practical (making garments, working a loom). They may be technical or scientific, understanding the materials from which textiles are made and understanding the machinery that is used to make them. But these skills separately do not make up the whole picture of textiles; for textiles to be successful – to give you the clothes you want, and to give industry the products it wants – all these different parts of the textiles business have to be put together. We sum that up in one word – design.

Design means producing the right product for the job. It is not just creating a pretty picture, getting a nice style, making the garment washable; design is a blend of all those things, it is taking into account all the various factors that go to make up a complete and usable textile item, and then putting them together to make it successful. This sometimes means that you have to give up some things in order to get others, in other words, you have to compromise. And all the time you have to do this within a price range that people can afford and will pay. If you don't get all these things right, the textile item you produce won't sell, and if nobody buys it you won't earn any money; if you are a firm, you will go bankrupt. Even if you make things at home for your own use, if they do not do what you intended you will have wasted the money you spent on buying fabric, trimmings, etc., and perhaps even the time which you might have spent more usefully elsewhere.

So the whole subject of textiles is about designing.

Within that overall description there are people who have particular skills and are specialists in the various aspects of design. These may be stylists, who are concerned with line, fashion and colour; or they may be technologists, that is, people who use scientific and technical knowledge and apply it to design machinery, or who make new fibres or test performance properties.

In all parts of the industry there are buyers and sellers. How does the system work? Well, think of the chain of processes from fibre through to the final customer. Take fibres, for example; in this area there will be some people whose job it is to sell fibres to the textile manufacturer, who spins them into yarn. The textile manufacturer will employ people as buyers, that is, those who negotiate with the sellers of the fibre industry to make sure they get the right products; and so on, all the way down the chain. When you come to retailing, the buyers are particularly important: they buy from clothing manufacturers and sell to you, the customer. And you, the customer, are again, of course, a buyer.

Buyers and sellers are not just people who haggle about money. You do not go into a shop and buy clothes on the basis of money alone, so a good buyer and good seller are those who are not concerned only about the price, but also understand the product they are buying. In other words, they understand about design. The best buyers are those who are not only good at getting a good price, but understand about style, performance testing and fashion, as well as what fibres perform best, so they know that the product they buy is right for the people they are going to try to sell it to. That means they can talk to designers to make sure that they develop the right product, and perhaps that is not available at the moment.

Jobs

Many people work in textiles, and they do a great variety of jobs. All contribute various skills to the overall aim of designing the right product and presenting it to the customer in such a way that the customer will buy it.

Because everybody buys clothes and uses textiles in one form or another, there are many job opportunities. Estimates vary, but as much as 15 per cent of the total workforce is engaged in work that is in some way connected with textiles. The chain starts with the fibre producers, and ends with the people who work in the retail outlets.

Let's look at some of these jobs in more detail.

Fibres

Of course, some fibres are produced by farmers or growers. But natural fibre production in the UK is very limited, and farming is a very specialized (and often a family) business.

Man-made fibre producers, however, are very different. They are mostly chemical companies, and employ people who have qualifications in chemistry or textiles. They also, however, employ people who are particularly interested in selling and promoting fibres to customers.

Although fibre producers seem a long way from the final product – clothes, or some other finished textile item – they carry out what is known as 'back selling'. That is, they employ people who promote (market) their products to all sections of the industry, including the final customer. Here, they look for people who have a more general knowledge of textiles – those who have specialized in business studies, perhaps with the emphasis on marketing and advertising.

Textiles

In the textiles industry, a wide variety of employees is needed. More than anything, the industry needs designers with a knowledge of textiles. But design, as we have seen, is not just making an attractive, artistic pattern, it involves a knowledge of the technical and commercial sides, if you are to be a successful designer and make things that people will buy, as opposed to creating pretty pictures which you might like. For these sorts of jobs, a design qualification is needed, but many of the design courses concentrate only on the artistic aspects, and these are becoming less and less popular with employers. What they are looking for are people who have attended design courses which include technical and business studies.

The textiles business also requires technologists. These are people who have specialized in the scientific and technical aspects of the industry.

Finally, the industry also needs people who can market or sell the products all over the world.

Clothing

The clothing industry has suffered from its 'rag trade' image, but it is a very big employer, and has a great need for people with design and management skills.

Designers are needed here, too, and again it is not enough just to understand fashion; you must be able to create patterns, select the right fabrics, and know how these are made up in the factory at an economic cost. In addition, the clothing industry is beginning to use more and more machinery – not just the old sewing machine – and it also needs technologists to help develop that area.

Retail

In the UK, the textile retailers are some of the biggest and most powerful firms in the country. They recruit people at all levels, from shop assistants to trainee managers, and they also employ buyers. They, too, look for designers, but with sound commercial sense, who can develop into buyers. They look for technologists who can ensure that the products they sell reach the right technical standard, and who can even go out and help their suppliers to get things right. And, of course, they employ people to run their stores at all levels.

Consumers and customers

We sometimes distinguish between consumers and customers. The customer is the person who actually *buys* the goods, while the consumer is the one who *uses* them (for example, parents buying for their children, or somebody buying a present for someone else). This can, of course, make a retailer's job a little difficult, because what attracts the customer may not please the consumer (again, parents buying for children). But one thing is certain – we all have a job for life as customers and consumers of textiles.

Figures estimate that on average people spend one sixth of their disposable income (the money they have for themselves after paying taxes and insurance, etc.) on textiles. That is a lot, and it is well worth spending it sensibly. If you know something about textiles, you should be in a better position to do just that.

If you design and make your own textile items, you will get more satisfaction from them, and since you will probably buy some of the basic materials, you will choose more sensibly how you spend your money.

Finally, if you have a problem, you should know your legal rights and be able to get either your money back or a replacement item. But remember, if you use your knowledge and buy carefully in the first place, you can avoid a great deal of irritation and inconvenience.

Acknowledgements

The Publishers would like to thank the following for permission to use their photographs:

Page 4 Justin Munroe; 5 Camera Press; 6 *top* Camera Press *bottom left* Justin Munroe *bottom right* Camera Press; 7 Camera Press; 8 *top* Camera Press *bottom* David Pratt; 11 Robert Harding Picture Library; 12 Camera Press; 15 Shirley Institute; 16 *top* Shirley Institute; 17 Courtaulds Limited; 19 ICI; 22 Justin Munroe; 24 International Institute for Cotton; 25 *top left* International Wool Secretariat *bottom right* International Wool Secretariat; 26 Shirley Institute; 28 International Institute for Cotton; 29 *bottom left and right* International Institute for Cotton; 30 David Pratt; 31 International Institute for Cotton; 32 *top* International Institute for Cotton *bottom* Shirley Institute; 33 *bottom left and right* International Institute for Cotton; 34 International Wool Secretariat; 37 Wycombe Marsh Paper Mills Limited; 39 *top* International Wool Secretariat *bottom* Shirley Institute, *bottom right* David Pratt; 54 *bottom* Ibis Manufacturing Limited; 55 Hoffman Supplies; 60 *top* Brintons Limited *bottom* Robert Harding Picture Library; 62 *top* David Pratt *middle* Hoverspeed, *bottom* RFD Company Limited; 63 *bottom* Vascutek; 65 *left* David Pratt *top right* Mary Evans Picture Library, *bottom right* St Ursula's Convent School; 68 *top* Robert Harding Picture Library *bottom left* National Magazine Company, *bottom right* Mary Evans Picture Library; 69 *top left* National Magazine Company, *bottom right* Justin Monroe, Philidar UK Ltd, *top right* Robert Harding Picture Library; 70 *top* David Pratt *bottom* Osborne and Little; 71 *top* National Magazine Company, *bottom* The Photographers' Library; 75 International Wool Secretariat; 76 International Institute for Cotton; 78 *top* International Institute for Cotton; 81 Barnaby's; 82 David Pratt; 99 James H Heal & Company Limited; 100 International Wool Secretariat; 101 Justin Monroe; 104 *top* Shirley Institute *bottom* David Pratt; 105 *bottom* Leslie Hubble Limited; 110 Hoechst UK Limited; 112 Justin Monroe; 131 International Wool Secretariat; 132 International Wool Secretariat.

The extracts from BS2747:1986 are reproduced by permission of BSI. Complete copies can be purchased from them at Linford Wood, Milton Keynes, MK1X 6LE.

Index